THE DIVINING HEART

THE DIVINING HEART

Dowsing and Spiritual Unfoldment

✳

Patricia C. and Richard D. Wright

Destiny Books
Rochester, Vermont

Destiny Books
One Park Street
Rochester, Vermont 05767

Library of Congress Cataloging-in-Publication Data
Wright, Patricia C.
The divining heart : dowsing and spiritual unfoldment / Patricia C. and Richard
D. Wright.
p. cm.
Includes bibliographical references and index.
ISBN 0-89281-423-3
1. Dowsing.   2. Spiritual life—Miscellanea.
I. Wright, Richard D., 1933–   .   II. Title.
BF1628.W75 1994
133.3'23—dc20   93-41713
CIP

Printed and bound in the United States

10 9 8 7 6 5 4 3 2 1

Text design by Leslie Bailey and Virginia Scott

Destiny Books is a division of Inner Traditions International

Distributed to the book trade in Canada by Publishers Group West (PGW),
Montreal West, Quebec

Distributed to the book trade in the United Kingdom by Deep Books, London

Distributed to the book trade in Australia by Millennium Books,
Newtown, N. S. W.

Distributed to the book trade in New Zealand by Tandem Press, Auckland,
New Zealand

CONTENTS

FOREWORD

"Coming events," according to the eighteenth-century poet Thomas Campbell, "cast their shadows before."

If we apply this perception to the growing darkness of planetary consciousness, we would seem to be in for an uncertain future. Every level of human thought and activity is being stressed beyond endurance. Confusion and confrontation are the order of the day in personal, national, and international relationships. How possibly can the outcome of such worldwide disharmony be other than damaging and destructive to everyone and to every nation?

Are we indeed, to use a phrase from this insightful book, "all Noah with the ark"? Drifting before the gathering storm and hostage to a future that by any measure of time and space seems devoid of the dynamic of hope?

The chapters that follow, firmly and gently, help us to navigate the turmoil that prevails upon us and point the way to the safe haven of the heart. This is the heart that is centered in its own divine wisdom and in the love for all creation that flows from it. Differing from other books of this kind, it gives definite and specific suggestions and directions for finding our way to the center of quietness and power and provides us with the safeguards that will keep us secure.

If the centered heart is our true destination, Pat and Dick

Wright have given us the means to reach and to know it. Its ways, they indicate, are not past manifesting, for it can resonate with all living things and, in so doing, align us with our role as cocreators instructed and empowered by caring and love.

Their theme, justly entitled *The Divining Heart*, is the one most needed in the world today, and we may take courage from their insight and compassion as we make our own way to the center and the safe harbor that is out of the swing of the sea.

T. Edward Ross 2nd

PREFACE

Among dowsing's many uses is that it is a tool that can help us to become more fully realized as human beings. Through bringing about changes in our perceptions of the world and of ourselves, dowsing can help us to become in harmony with what we understand to be the intelligence—the insight—of the heart. Although the wish to be of service may have been the original motivation to learn to dowse, the best service ultimately may be understood to be the change—the *unfoldment*—that occurs within the dowser's own awareness. It is through this change that dowsers can begin to affect the consciousness of others—and indeed the nature of everything in their surroundings.

We understand the *heart* here to mean the subtle heart, part of the subtle anatomy of the human being—the heart that "produces true knowledge, comprehensive intuition, the gnosis . . . of God and the divine mysteries."[1] By the title *The Divining Heart* we suggest the benefit of unfolding the skills of dowsing in a way that is centered in and guided by the subtle heart that is understood to be at the center of all harmonious thought and action.

We approach the divining heart through the seven-stage paradigm presented in *The Divining Mind*. As discussed there, a dowser's growing awareness of underlying unity occurs concurrently with the refinement of dowsing skills. Levels of increasing subtlety, complexity, and responsibility are unfolded as the dowser moves through the stages.

We intend this book to be a continuation of *The Divining Mind*, and so we begin with a brief overview of the beginning stages of dowsing before concentrating on the later stages. Our intention is to establish a conceptual framework for understanding the succession of stages and to describe some ways in which dowsing can help us to uncover our true human potential, including our role as caretakers of our earth home and of our fellow beings on the planet.

In the list of recommended readings we suggest a number of sources and books that we have found helpful in our learning.

Our sincere thanks go to editor-in-chief Leslie Colket, to Cannon Labrie, and to the rest of the staff at Inner Traditions International for seeing this book through from manuscript to final publication.

We feel very grateful for and thank all the spiritual teachers and dowsers, known and unknown, on this plane and on others, who have shared their knowledge and understanding. Particularly we wish to express gratitude to the being of Khidr and for those timeless teachers of the religion of love—the religion of the heart—Muhyiddin Ibn 'Arabi, Jalaluddin Rumi, and Hazrat Inayat Khan. For their living presence and guidance, our special thanks go to Pir Vilayat Inayat Khan, Reshad Feild, and also to Atum O'Kane and Kabir Helminski. We are also deeply grateful for the friendship and teaching of that grand master of dowsing, T. Edward (Terry) Ross 2nd. And for their companionship with lessons along the way, we thank the dear four-footeds Sean and Brigit. All praise and thanks to God for all these teachers, and apologies if we have fallen short in our understanding of the richness we have been given.

INTRODUCTION

Nearly two decades ago we were part of a crowd in the basement of a church in Danville, Vermont. It was Saturday morning of the annual dowsers' convention and we were attending a beginners' class led by a rugged, older Down-Easterner. He located underground veins of water and showed us how a variety of dowsing instruments responded to them. Questions arose. He listened to each one with patience, looking directly at the questioner, and then answered, sometimes with a personal anecdote and other times with more detailed explanations. Then he invited us all to try hands-on for ourselves. Soon he showed Dick how to hold a Y-rod, that plastic device that has replaced the old forked stick, and aimed him toward the target. There was no response. Dick felt a twinge of disappointment. The old gentleman gave him an amused glance and said, "Here, I'll do it with you." Again Dick held the Y-rod, only this time the teacher placed his hand on one of Dick's hands. They walked toward the target, and the rod moved. He let go; another try alone and the rod moved again. From then on, the rod moved every time. "Now you've got it," he said, as if to a slow student who had finally solved a problem correctly. "Practice, and you'll do okay." Later we learned that this teacher was kindly, self-effacing Gordon MacLean, a chemical engineer who had learned to dowse in his later years. He was not as

1

famous as fellow Maine dowser Henry Gross, but then Henry appeared in three books by Kenneth Roberts. Gordon did write "A Field Guide to Dowsing," a practical booklet that still holds up well after nearly three decades.

About one decade ago we were sitting in a pew near the back of a church in Derby Line, Vermont, this time with master dowser Terry Ross and his wife Ginny. We all held L-rods, bent metal rods with plastic sleeves. "I want you to imagine that there's an underground vein of flowing water directly under the back of the pew in front of us," said Terry. "Get the picture of it in your mind. Now hold the rods and lean toward the pew —don't dowse the pew; dowse the vein." We all leaned forward, and the rods moved. "What were we dowsing?" Terry asked. "Where was the target?"

"That's the idea I want to get across in the dowsing school," he said later that evening in our living room. "The dowsing doesn't take place out there; it takes place in your mind. We didn't dowse a vein of water; we dowsed the *idea* of a vein of water. That's what happens whenever we dowse. It's a mental activity. We create the idea of a target, and we create resonance with the actual target out there."

During the next four years Dick and Terry developed this concept of dowsing as a mental activity involving resonance with a target through a series of dowsing schools that preceded the annual conventions of the American Society of Dowsers in Danville, Vermont. This concept of dowsing fit comfortably into recent theories of physics, biology, and brain-mind studies. It also received verification from those scientists, engineers, psychologists, doctors, and medical practitioners who attended those four dowsing schools. Students at the schools checked their progress in learning to dowse immediately verifiable targets with field instructors (Pat was one of these instructors). When the schools were completed, the ideas expressed in them became the basis for *The Divining Mind*, the predecessor to this book.

In addition to giving practical advice and suggesting verifiable exercises for beginners, *The Divining Mind* also examined the nature of this dowsing paradigm and suggested that one's skill in dowsing is best developed through seven stages, with each stage emerging from the one before it and preparing the dowser for the one that follows it. That book took the reader through the first three stages—on-site, up-to-the-horizon, and over-the-horizon dowsing—and into the fourth, the stage of "knowing" that is the interface between passive and active dowsing.

We encourage you to read and study *The Divining Mind* for its full coverage of the beginning stages of dowsing and background information for understanding further stages. This book will concentrate on the more advanced stages, enlarging upon the basic idea that all dowsing occurs as an activity of the mind. Once one learns to dowse, one's subsequent skill does not depend on the particular device used, nor on the material from which it is made, nor on its shape. The dowsing tool is simply a readout device, and the dowser chooses the particular device most appropriate to his or her needs in a given situation. Development of skill depends not only on practical experience but also on a person's mental capacity. As part of his or her dowsing education, certain personal rituals may be developed, but the information being transmitted through the movements of the dowsing device already exists in the mind of the dowser, through resonance with the information being sought. We further suggest that the development of the advanced stages corresponds to a similar conscious unfoldment of qualities of the subtle heart—the center of spiritual activity and growth.

Over a decade ago we began a nonprofit teaching center, grounded in the unifying beliefs at the heart of the world's great spiritual traditions and in the understanding that an individual's spiritual nature unfolds through stages, after barriers imposed by a limited sense of self are gradually removed. Ongoing classes have included studies in sound and music, nature and the natural kingdoms, teachings of the great masters, as well as meditation techniques, breathing exercises, and practice in sacred sounds that open centers in the subtle body and help to unfold as yet unrealized potentials.

We realized very soon that this spiritual focus provided both grounding and context for dowsing, and also that the later stages of dowsing harmonized with similar stages of spiritual realization and could most effectively be unfolded within this context. We feel that all aspects of existence, on this plane and on the more subtle ones, are aspects of the Divine, and that the goal of the dowser—in concert with that of the spiritual seeker—is to live and move in harmony with the Source.

PART ONE

THE REACH OF MIND: STAGES ONE THROUGH FOUR

✳

And I say unto you, Ask, and it shall be given you;
seek, and ye shall find;
knock, and it shall be opened unto you.
For every one that asketh receiveth;
and he that seeketh findeth;
and to him that knocketh it shall be opened.

—*Luke 11: 9–10*

1

THE FIRST STEPS

When we dowse we create the idea of the target, whether that target is tangible or intangible. The accuracy of our response, or indeed whether we get a response at all, depends on the degree of resonance our creation achieves with the desired target.

—*T. Edward Ross 2nd and Richard D. Wright*

Everyone has the innate ability to learn to dowse, an ability as old as humankind, even though few people understand the potential of the dowsing process and fewer still recognize its implications and responsibilities. Although everyone has dowsing ability in potential, this ability is usually unrecognized and undeveloped. And few understand dowsing's usefulness as a tool to access intuition.

After we learn the basics of how to dowse and have some practice, we naturally feel the need to understand exactly what it is that we have been doing, but it is better if we have this understanding from the beginning. The quotation at the beginning of the chapter is in essence the paradigm we use in this book: that all dowsing, no matter what its nature may be, occurs as an activity of the mind.

Most people who have heard of dowsing associate it primarily with the finding of water with a forked stick. They think of a dowser as someone with special psychic ability. When they hear that dowsing can be used in ways other than for locating water, they may become curious enough to ask, "Well, what exactly *is* dowsing? How do you define it?"

Most definitions of dowsing create at best only limited understanding. They have been how-to (but don't ask how it works), circular (without really saying anything—the dictionary definitions), related to one's sensitivity to radiations (but don't ask how this applies to map dowsing), and so on.

We define *dowsing* as *the process of discovering or uncovering information through the medium of the self*, understanding that the nature of information received through dowsing varies for each successive level of dowsing activity. Locating a vein of water on-site, for example, is not the same as pinpointing it on a map or perceiving it through deviceless dowsing. When we advance in our ability and turn to the world within to gain information, that world becomes a mirror of the world outside and we learn to see each of these "worlds" as reflecting the other.

A *tool* is simply *whatever one uses to accomplish a job*. For most dowsers, this tool may be a pendulum, a Y-rod, or an L-rod. Not only are objects or devices tools, however; so is the process itself. Thus, a person may have a finely developed skill, and that skill is a tool that the person uses to carry out a complex job. We will therefore keep in mind that "tool" means more than simply an external physical device. In deviceless dowsing, external tools are put aside and the dowser's body then becomes the tool. The response occurs as a sensory or muscular event: a feeling of warmth or pressure on the hand, for example, or an involuntary twitch of the fingers. In intuitive dowsing, unconscious processes become the tool: the dowser experiences a "knowing" beyond the senses.

Two other terms we use are *spiritual* and *unfoldment*. We define *spiritual* in two stages: *the realization of the Reality behind the interconnectedness of all aspects of existence, both known and unknown,* and *the acceptance of one's personal relationship and responsibility to this Reality as it is expressed through this interconnectedness.* The unfoldment of this realization is the goal of any steps we take toward personal unfoldment and thus must be kept in mind at every stage of our progress.

We use the term *unfoldment* (rather than *development*) to suggest the process of manifestation as described by physicist David Bohm. Briefly, Bohm calls the world of everyday reality the explicate order, while the implicate order is a more subtle realm of vibrational reality from which come all things that manifest in the explicate order. Everything that will or can manifest already exists in potential in a more subtle state as vibration, creating patterns of interaction with everything else enfolded within the implicate order, from which specific things unfold and become manifest in coherent patterns at the appropriate time, as part of the reality of our everyday world. The implication is that the essential aspect of one's spiritual nature already exists, enfolded as potentiality within every cell of each person's being; our responsibility becomes that of allowing it to unfold and to become a conscious part of us—our "God consciousness"—in everyday reality.

Dowsing, like gardening or housekeeping, is simply a process or activity. Any such activity may be used as a tool toward spiritual unfoldment if it is undertaken from the appropriate perspective. With right awareness and intent an activity can become the outer expression of spiritual unfoldment, a metaphor for something more subtle. The cultivation of one's garden then relates to the cultivation of one's spiritual growth; the cleaning and ordering of a house become akin to internal spiritual cleaning and ordering. In a Zen story, a student asks his teacher what he did before he reached enlightenment. The teacher answers, "I chopped wood and carried water." "And after you reached enlightenment?" asks the student, to which the teacher answers, "I chopped wood and carried water." It is the same external activity, but to those able to understand, it has been transformed by the teacher's evolved state of consciousness.

Although the dowsing process is popularly thought of as a way to locate external targets or to identify physical causes of distress, these are only part of its potential. Also, the clarity of a result achieved, especially through the more advanced stages of dowsing, relates directly to the clarity of the awareness of the dowser. We can learn to become successful at more subtle aspects of dowsing to the extent that we become aware of more subtle aspects of our own selves. Part of this process involves the dowser's willingness, not so much to learn new things as to unlearn old things, or at least to reintegrate those old things into a broader perspective.

At one time scientists tended to view the universe around them, including their own personal universes, as composed of separate objects, as parts in a machine. Contemporary scientific thinking no longer views the universe as a collection of separate objects, but more as a web of relationships and habits emerging from wave patterns that, when involved with a variety of interference patterns, unfold into our reality as the atomic structures that form what we perceive as solid matter.

This creation of forms has its correspondence in the holographic process. In that process a coherent beam of light is passed through a photographic negative that appears composed of random, chaotic swirls of interference patterns. These patterns, however, unfold into an organized, seemingly three-dimensional form in space. One can see this form and even receive a dowsing response to it. Moreover, if the holographic "picture" includes in it a magnifying glass, then as one looks from different angles through it at other parts of the picture, the holographic magnifying glass will magnify those other parts of the holographic image. It is as if the picture has a reality of its own, even though one can pass a hand through or walk through it. Even if a small piece of the negative is cut apart and then a coherent beam of light (one of a narrow waveband) is passed through it, the entire holographic image will appear, although less clearly than it did with the original whole negative.

We do not ordinarily see the world around us as a holographic world; it is a world perceived through lenses, not only those of our eyes but also of the receptors of all our seemingly different sensory systems. This is the perception of David Bohm's explicate order, the manifested order we accept as our everyday reality. We are accustomed to those lenses, for they objectify and bring details into sharp focus and strengthen our awareness of relationships. Through lenses we establish our worldview, and conventional scientists develop their thinking in lenslike terms of analysis and synthesis. It is difficult for us to move to any additional kind of thinking beyond analysis and synthesis because this is the only kind of thinking to which we have become accustomed in a lifetime of training.

If we are to understand dowsing as a tool for gaining access to more subtle aspects of ourselves, we must develop its use gradually and systematically through a series of stages that include, but go beyond, the closed paradigm of lens systems. To us, the system most useful, open-ended, and nonconstricting is the seven-stage process originally suggested by Terry Ross and included in *The Divining Mind.* In this system the dowser masters skills for each stage sequentially and in ways that can be verified.

Before beginning your search for actual targets, you become familiar with two common dowsing tools. L-rods are metal rods about a foot long with additional lengths at right angles that serve as handles. The handles are usually enclosed in plastic sleeves, so that the rods may be held securely yet still be free to rotate. An L-rod is held in each hand, so that the longer parts point away from you, parallel with the ground, as though they were six-shooters. You train yourself to have them swing away from each other, at right angles, when you cross the target or for a "yes" response. A "no" response would be that they stay parallel and unmoving.

The other tool, the Y-rod, is either a springy forked stick or two rods of stiff plastic tied together at one end. To use the Y-rod, you hold the other ends securely in your upturned palms so that the stem of the rod points upward, away from you, at about a forty-five degree angle and with as much tension in the rod as you can create. Then you train yourself to let it swing downward when you cross over, or otherwise locate, a target. That would be the "yes" response; a "no" response would be no movement.

The first stage of dowsing is to locate a target on-site. Try to form a vivid image of the target—a vein of water or a water pipe. At first the target should be one you can easily verify. With that image in mind, you then walk across a field or room and request that the tool respond when you are directly over the target. At first the response may be only approximate, but with practice accuracy increases. You will find that your accuracy and precision depend on two factors: first, that what you are seeking is clear and precise; and second, that the image you create corresponds to the target you seek. A suitable programming in your mind, as you seek the target, might be, "Please show me, by the 'yes' response of the rods, if there is here a year-around flowing vein of water, less than two hundred feet deep, with a quality of eight or better (ten being best), that will yield at least five gallons per minute, and that can be drilled into without problems."

The question at first seems complicated, but your brain learns to sort it all out and orchestrates the appropriate "yes" or "no" response through your dowsing tool. You then can walk along, asking that the rods open in the "yes" response when you are over the center of the target.

Even though you may be a beginner, think of your progress in dowsing as following the path of a spiral. Picture, for example, the cross section of a chambered nautilus: its spiral becomes larger with each turning until finally it opens outward and "home" becomes infinite. As you master the first stage of dowsing—even if you stay with it for years, with targets of increasing complexity—you are still primarily working with skills appropriate to the first turn of the spiral.

At the first stage you learn to locate a target and ask further questions to determine specific information about it and to distinguish it from similar targets. Your questions are framed in the binary—yes or no—manner of a computer, and you must be able to interpret yes and no responses from the movement of the tools. We have described the responses usually interpreted as yes and no, but you may develop another system, so long as the responses are clear and consistent.

The dowsing device you are using is a tool, in the same way that a hammer or an automobile or a computer is a tool. An experienced carpenter routinely uses a hammer with accuracy and efficiency, just as an experienced automobile driver can thread his way confidently through complex roadways and traffic patterns that would terrify a beginner. A computer whiz can design a house in intricate detail as fingers translate thoughts through the keyboard. The carpenter wants to pound nails; he probably doesn't want to design a whole housing complex. Nevertheless, he knows that a design does exist, and he pounds his nails in places appropriate to that design. In dowsing, it is also important to be aware of a larger picture. A beginning dowser doesn't need to know all about chaos theory or quantum physics, but he or she should know that such theories exist and that it may become appropriate down the line to learn more about them. Expecting a beginner to know how dowsing works is like expecting a dependable carpenter with no computer knowledge to know how a computer-assisted design program works. It is why we emphasize that dowsing is a skill learned and mastered in stages and that each stage requires comprehension of additional concepts that then enlarge the framework within which understanding may grow, as appropriate for the next stage.

The second stage of dowsing includes targets found up-to-the-horizon. One may look, for example, for the best site for a well on a piece of property. To scan the horizon, grasp an L-rod in your dominant hand, holding your arm straight out from the shoulder, so that the tool becomes an extension of your arm. You then form the appropriate mental image of the target, ask that the tool show you where it is, and slowly move your arm in an arc until the tool seems to "lock on" to the direction of the target. You note what lies in the line of sight in that precise direction and then repeat the process from a position some distance away. This is the process of triangulation, and the location of your target will be at the point where the two lines of sight would cross. If you use a Y-rod, you would hold the tool and scan the horizon; the Y-rod would dip downward in the appropriate direction.

If you have practiced the second stage so that you can locate targets with consistent, verifiable accuracy, then you are ready for the third stage, which includes targets beyond your sight—indeed, targets anywhere on earth. Usually dowsers work with a map of the target area to discover the required information. After you clearly know what questions you will be asking and you form a clear image of the target, you may then find the approximate location of that target either by scanning and triangulation from the edge of the map or by moving a straightedge across the map from side to side and from top to bottom, noting where the yes response of the dowsing tool occurs. The dowsed lines cross at the general location of the target. For this kind of dowsing, most dowsers use a pendulum, the device we will present in detail in chapter 3.

After sufficient practice using these tools, some dowsers develop the confidence to train their hands or fingers to act as tools. The movement may be a specific twitch of the fingers, or it may be a feeling of heat or pressure as the hand reaches the point of response.

It becomes increasingly clear, especially when you dowse distant targets at this third stage, that although it is the device that moves, it is the "movement" in the mind that moves the device. A sophisticated metal detector can find metal on-site with a high degree of discrimination, but no matter how good it is, it can't map dowse.

If you are a musician you are familiar with overtones, those harmonic intervals that give richness to fundamental frequencies. Sometimes another object will produce a sound, or sympathetic vibration, that corresponds to an overtone of the note you produce. That other object vibrates, not directly to your note, but in resonance with an aspect of your note.

Any thought you create produces its own unique, subtle vibrations, complete with its own overtones, as a musical note does no matter what instrument creates it. Likewise, everything that exists produces unique, subtle vibrations appropriate to itself. When you dowse while holding the image of the target in mind, your aim is that these vibrations may then create resonance with various harmonics and overtones of vibrations basic to that particular target, no matter where it is located.

After you have mastered the first stage of dowsing and know how to use the tools, your mind then has the capacity to begin the conscious training necessary for mastery of the succeeding stages. At the second and third stages, where a thought, question, or image must be clearly established, you can learn to go through a complex interplay of dowsing tool and mental image resonating with the target. At that stage, as with an experienced driver steering through traffic, this tremendously complex process may seem effortless.

Progressing through the first three stages, the dowser learns to establish increasingly subtle levels of affinity with the target. First comes the idea of the target, held in the dowser's mind. An image or intent is created there, and to the extent that that image is in resonance with the actual target, the dowser is able to discover its location and various facts about it. In stage one, the process is somewhat like that of a metal detector generating a clear signal when it is over a metal target. The stage-two process is more akin to that of a direction finder picking up a specific signal. As dowsing skills develop, the dowser also becomes more sensitive to increasingly subtle levels of resonance. When the idea of a target is created, a degree of resonance may be created with the actual target, somewhat as a shortwave receiver may resonate with a specific signal halfway around the world. The brain becomes trained to detect and identify a particular target with verifiable success. At this point, after sufficient practice at the first three stages, the dowser may be ready to progress to stage four.

One of the skills at stage four is to move beyond the usual dowsing devices, including the physical senses; that is, the dowser often "knows" the response before the device indicates it.

As your ease and accuracy increase, you may comment to a friend, "You know, when I'm dowsing, I sometimes know what the answer will be before the dowsing rod (or pendulum) swings." This "knowing" is a clue that you have now progressed to the fourth stage of dowsing. The act of dowsing now becomes an act of knowing; an unconscious reflexive response is being transformed into a state of conscious awareness.

At first the knowing arises unexpectedly and only occasionally, but then gradually it develops with more certainty and seems independent of the strictly left-brain or rational workings of the mind. As with conventional dowsing in the first three stages, confidence and trust in this knowing can develop most successfully when whatever is being known can be verified objectively. When results can be corroborated consistently, then the external dowsing tool becomes a convenience rather than a necessity.

This fourth stage, or fourth turning of the spiral of mastery, is a critical stage of transition. So far we have been talking about verifiable dowsing responses that occur as a result of increasingly subtle levels of resonance with given targets. To be more precise, it is response to an extremely dense interference pattern of vibrations. Everything in existence—from passing thought to spiral galaxy—is created and maintained through the process of resonance.

We know that *vibration* is a term loosely used in connection with wave forms or back-and-forth particle motion. It is also, however, used to indicate a complex, systematic modulation of time. To put it simply, both time and location are brought into existence as results of vibration. Our universe exists as a result of intricate, fixed habits of vibration, and these habits create a sense of time and place that is shared by everything in the universe, including ourselves. As we begin to gain mastery of the fourth stage of dowsing, we are now at a juncture at which we may pass the threshold of the here-and-now and create resonance with other places and times.

A skill unfolded at this stage is the ability to obtain answers to nonphysical and abstract questions, as well as to ignore limitations of space and time, such as in asking if a vein of water at a location in another state will flow actively year round, or discovering not only the location but the date of an artifact at a distant archaeological dig.

As with those earlier stages, dowsing at this stage often can be verified. For example, you may dowse an archaeological site and check your information against later findings. At first the dowsed answers may well be random, but, as with those responses obtained during the early days of dowsing at stage one, accuracy does improve over time.

Most dowsers can eventually reach this stage even though its mastery requires more patience to unfold than do the preceding stages. If the dowser is to move beyond this stage, however, there must be a complementary unfolding of spiritual awareness. Without this awareness the personal ego could be thrown off balance and develop either a false sense of personal power or a condition of physical disharmony.

As the fourth stage—the interface stage—unfolds, the dowser may begin to interact actively with information received at a level corresponding to its subtlety. This realization leads naturally to stage five, where the dowser may cooperate with nature in a limited manner. The dowser, for example, may request, after receiving all the permissions, that a vein of water be moved in a specified way and have this occur, not by the dowser's physical intervention but as a result of the request itself. When this begins to happen regularly, then the dowsing request is not only a totally mental act but has become a prayer. The dowser may discover and identify a disharmonious situation such as a noxious energy field. After assessing the situation, he or she then requests permissions (described in chapter 2) and, if these are received, asks that the disharmonious situation be brought into harmony. As the false sense of limited ego begins to let go of its illusion of self-importance, and as spiritual awareness grows, one's relationship with nature or with a given target within nature will enlarge to increasingly subtle levels. The dowser may then be able to become consciously involved with the process of creation itself. When this happens, the dowser has reached stage six, the level of cocreation with nature, and may, after having received all the permissions, suggest and bring about the rearrangement of forces emerging from the implicate order to result in changes in the natural world. This may happen, for example, during some forms of distant healing of plant, animal, or human being, including changes in basic genetic structure.

Dowsers may develop some capability in these six levels after an appropriate period of outer practice, inner training, and patience, but we feel that the combination of dowsing skills with skills of an authentic spiritual discipline allows for the most harmonious unfoldment of each stage. Some dowsers may then briefly be able to reach the next stage. At stage seven the skills mastered in stages five and six are used reflexively, beyond conscious awareness and in attunement with the ongoing flow of creation from the implicate order. In time this level may begin to unfold on its own, if and when the student is ready. It is the level of the great mystics and spiritual masters, known and unknown; it is an ideal toward which some dowsers aspire.

2

RESPONSIBILITY

When a dowser moves from passive gathering of information (up through stage-four dowsing) to making requests for changes based on information dowsed (stages five and six), he or she must become aware of the responsibility incurred.

We understand that "responsible" means being reliable, trustworthy, able to distinguish right from wrong, and that it involves accountability.

The intention of the code of ethics of the American Society of Dowsers is that the dowser should have not only integrity but also dignity and modesty, should not promise what cannot be produced, and should not claim that joining a dowsing society makes anyone a competent dowser. These are surely very basic aspects of what it means to be a responsible dowser.

Beyond all this, however, is the sense of responsibility that comes from the recognition of the Unity that connects all beings and all things. "Thou canst not pluck a flower without the troubling of a star," wrote Thomas Traherne, and it really appears to be so. The term *butterfly effect* is used in modern chaos theory to indicate that what appears unimportant may not be: the beating of a butterfly's wings in China may cause a fluctuation in weather across the world. There is pattern in everything, even in what appears to be chaos.

This sense of interconnectedness means that if you are

asked to dowse for a place to have a well drilled or dug, then you want to find "the best possible place" for that well. An old-time dowser walked across a field with a forked stick, looking just for underground water. Now, thanks to all those dowsers who have helped to refine the programming of our search, we know how to ask for precisely the best spot, for example, for a well of pure drinking water with a year-round flow of at least five gallons per minute at less than two hundred feet deep. And we have learned to ask questions to determine the hardness or softness of the water, whether any of the streams crossing at the well site have undesirable qualities (such as contamination with sulphur or arsenic or too much iron), and we can ask precisely the depth of the veins. We can dowse anything, so long as we can conceptualize and frame the questions in the yes/no mode of the computer.

In addition to the matters mentioned so far, we want to be aware of the interconnection of all beings and all things. We know that as good neighbors we would want to be sure that a vein we tapped for a well would not mean that our neighbor's supply would be seriously depleted. And we would want to be particularly careful of this before making any changes, such as in diverting (moving) any veins. But also we would want to be aware of how our actions might affect trees, plants, animals, birds, and other parts of the environment. Because we can't possibly think of all the ramifications of any act, we always stress the idea of asking permission. As a first step, that means permission from the custodian of the land. In part that is respect for privacy. We wouldn't go into people's houses without being invited or having been given permission to be there, and we don't go onto their land or into their inner spaces without permission. We must be asked by or have permission from the custodian of the land before we dowse, and especially before we make any changes affecting the land. Notice that we say permission from the *custodian*, for ownership of the land is really a fiction; the land was here before us and we trust will endure long after our time here. As we understand it, our charge while we are here on earth is to be custodians of the earth and of her life.

Once we have the permission of the steward of an individual piece of land, however, we have not finished; we then must ask the three permission questions that we were taught and that we always teach as an integral part of dowsing. These permission questions are: May I? (Am I permitted by That which allows me to dowse to do so?) Can I? (Am I able? Do I have enough skill for this job?) Should I? (Is this the time? Am I the one to do this?) We are dowsing the answers to these questions, so it is important to have mastered basic dowsing in order to get correct answers. When dowsing for these permissions, you are addressing something that gives you answers. Whether you want to consider this something to be God, your high self, your guides, your own true being—whatever "voice" speaks to you at this time for That which you consider to be the Highest and Truest and Best—that is the "authority" from whom you are asking the permissions through dowsing.

If you get "no" to any of the permission questions, pay attention. Sometimes this may mean that you have a personal ego interest and are not able to keep your own wishes or fears out of your response. It may mean that you haven't the skill, or that you don't have the information to frame cogent questions, or just that you are too tired to do the job at that time. You can ask when it would be appropriate—if it would be—to try again to dowse these questions. But sometimes "no" may mean that you are not the right one to do the job—or even that it is best not done at all.

Beginning dowsers naturally feel excitement at what they have learned and experience great desire to get out into the world and set wrong things right. But as you know, if you look back on situations about which you felt strongly in the past, sometimes your present view is very different indeed. It is presumptuous as a dowser to assume from your rational view that you always know what should and what should not be done. If you consider the world as a school and understand that we are here to grow spiritually, and that everyone else is here for that reason too, then sometimes it may not be to the highest good to change something that you in your present rational view would consider "bad." Sometimes that very situation is an important learning device for the person or persons involved.

Everything can be a teacher: a stone, a plant, an animal, a situation, even an illness. There are many forms of understanding, and someone so trained can read much about a person in the eyes, in the ears, in the face, on the feet, in the hands, in the posture, in the pulse. A landscape may be read also. When you learn how to read it, you find that the whole world is a book. Gradually we become more aware of "that which transpires behind that which appears," as the Sufis say. So if we are just interested in the surface of reality and try to correct everything on that level, we may be quite unaware of what is really happening out of our present range of understanding. So we ask the permissions, for we want to be helpers, not hinderers, in the Divine Plan.

If a dowser is truly responsible, he or she does not turn away from that responsible aspect of self after a particular dowsing search is completed. Experiments have indicated that certain brain-wave patterns hold whether experienced dowsers are doing a search or just saying hello. These patterns are similar to those of long-time meditators, an indication that experienced dowsers stay tuned to try to understand signals from the universe, even after specific dowsing jobs have been completed.

A responsible and trained dowser uses dowsing in daily life, when the permissions are received, to help toward the harmony and well-being of self, family, pets, and any land for which he or she is custodian. And eventually a dowser may be asked to help those beyond the immediate family.

If that dowser is you, you will want to be sure that by then you have fully absorbed the intent of ethical dowsing and that your contributions are truly toward the highest good. If you are sincerely asked for help, and believe that you have the capacity in a particular situation to give it, and you receive "yes" to not some but *all* of the permission questions, then you have to make your decision with a full sense of responsibility and accountability. Service, harmlessness, and harmony with the highest good are always the dowsing intent. Answers to permission questions help as prerequisites in making complex ethical decisions.

Ethical decisions are required in all dowsing matters, not just those related to healing. There is great diversity in the ways dowsers view dowsing for personal gain—for the stock market and for treasure, for example. Some dowse regularly for their own gain. You will have to determine what is appropriate for you.

The issue of whether or not to charge for dowsing, once one is experienced, is also an ethical decision. Many water, oil, and mineral dowsers charge a fair day's wage. Many do not, although they may accept expenses and, in lieu of a fee, suggest that a donation be made to a charitable or nonprofit organization. Many people do not value what is free, and it is important for them to make some kind of energy exchange for what is done. Again, individual dowsers must decide what is right for them, and this may be subject to change as their views evolve or as their life circumstances change.

There is never a charge, of course, for dowsing done as prayer.

Dowsing to find missing persons or animals is not always clear-cut. Does this animal or person wish to be found, or was it escaping from a situation for good reason? Asking this additional question may help you to understand why you may not have received a "yes" to a permission question.

By dowsing you can find where the deer are in the woods. This may be fun to know, but at hunting season is this an appropriate dowsing use if you, as a responsible steward, are asked by a hunter to find the deer?

What about dowsing in archaeology, or for minerals to be strip-mined in sacred lands? What about dowsing targets in the military?

Obviously, there are not pat answers to many ethical issues, and you, as a responsible dowser, must think carefully about what you will and will not do. The permissions may help to give you a perspective that you otherwise would not have.

Remember all the unquestioned assumptions with which we grew up? Learning to dowse means that it's time to re-evaluate these.

Do you think all environmental or animal rights groups are equally good and want to support them all? Dowse them in regard to whether or not they do what they say and how effective your contribution to them will be toward implementing the cause you care to support. Dowse your political candidates and those running for the school board. You can see that the potential of dowsing for information is vast and that responsible dowsing can help you to live with greater truth and effectiveness.

3

INFORMATION DOWSING: USING THE PENDULUM

We have so far briefly reviewed the use of L-rods and Y-rods. Another commonly used dowsing tool is the pendulum, the tool most often used for information dowsing—the kind of dowsing that we will need to be able to do as we progress. A pendulum is a suspended, balanced weight, of any material and of any size, that will swing freely and respond easily to your directions. You may make your own pendulum, using a fishing weight attached to the end of a string, a wooden ball hung from a fine chain, or any variation you choose, or you may prefer to purchase one. There's nothing magical about the pendulum; it's simply another tool.

Once you have your pendulum, the first step is to adapt it to your own rhythms—called tuning the pendulum. You hold the string or chain close to the weight with the thumb and first finger of your dominant hand. Move your hand to start the weight swinging back and forth. As you do this, let the string or chain out slowly to the point where the pendulum weight swings in a circle on its own. This spot on the string or chain will be a good point at which to hold that particular pendulum; it is a point at which we say the pendulum is "tuned."

Next, you again swing the pendulum back and forth and then ask it to indicate your "yes" response. Usually this is a clockwise swing in a full circle. If you get no response, gently "train" the pendulum by swinging the weight clockwise and saying, "This is yes." Repeat this from time to time until the response is learned. The pendulum is, of course, not being trained or learning anything, any more than a car learns how to drive through traffic, but you act as though it were, in order to remove your own conscious thoughts from the programming. In like manner, discover what is the response for "no." For most dowsers this is a counterclockwise swing. Again, if you don't get a natural response, swing the pendulum counterclockwise and say, "This is no." If the two responses are reversed, that is okay. Any convention that gives you a clear difference between your "yes" and your "no" is acceptable so long as it is consistent.

Particularly if you are a beginner, it is a good idea to check your yes and no responses before you dowse answers to any questions. Sometimes your body wants to reverse the responses. So long as you have a clear "yes" and "no," you can dowse; but you do need to know each time you dowse which response is which. Many people have trouble training themselves to produce subtle reflexive responses, whether it is in driving or in dowsing, so be aware that it may take you some time to get a clear dowsing response with a pendulum. Persevere!

Before we do any dowsing, using any tool, we first ask the permission questions. If we have been asked to dowse by someone else, then these questions are especially important, and, if we are being asked to "do" anything based on what we dowse, permission is absolutely critical. Also, if we are asked to dowse in regard to a person, that person (or someone closely related to that person) must make the initial request. (For the land, the custodian must give permission.) These are permissions given prior to, but not superseding, the three dowsed permission questions: May I? Can I? Should I?

If we have dowsed accurately and have received "yes" to all the permission questions, then we may proceed to dowse further, framing each question so that yes and no responses will be meaningful.

Learning to dowse is in major part learning to ask the right questions. This takes time and effort, and the more we know about a subject, the more precise our questions can be.

We have found that a great help in developing skill and accuracy in dowsing is to keep a dowsing journal. Note your progress, recording both when you are right and when you are wrong. When you do make a mistake, view it as an opportunity to learn why you made it. Did your hopes or fears or habits get in the way of the true response? Everyone makes mistakes, but it is important to note them, along with your successes, and then to use them as learning devices so that you will make fewer and fewer errors in the future. Don't give up, saying that you can't dowse. Patience is part of the learning. Again, persevere!

4

PUTTING DOWSING TO USE

To become a genuine dowser you need to dowse every day. If you are a beginner, you must develop a track record so that when you really need to be able to dowse you have confidence in your results. This means using dowsing not as a party game but to meet genuine needs, and doing it in ways that can be checked. This chapter will suggest how you can begin to develop your skill in a variety of everyday situations. (In the list of recommended readings are books to direct your further exploration of subjects lightly touched on here.)

You can practice on your own house, where you can dowse outside for the water and sewer lines and where they come into the house (as you learned to do in *The Divining Mind*) and can verify your dowsing by looking for these pipes in the cellar. Then ask your neighbors if you can dowse their houses, and again you will have confirmation of your dowsing, either because the neighbors know the location of those lines or because you can see them in their basements.

Those of you in houses with septic tanks that were installed before you moved in, and for which the location is unknown, will realize the value of this kind of dowsing if the septic system requires attention. Practice first at a house where the location of the septic tank is already known, so that you will be ready if your own tank needs to be found.

The same kind of practice can help you with your own water system. Where is the break in the water line from the spring? Can you pinpoint it or will you have to dig up the entire line? Obviously, if you can dowse the place to dig to find the break, you will be saving work or expense.

If you are building a new house, dowsing can also be a great help. You can sit in the real estate office (or, if you are still shy about having people watch you dowse, at home with a list) and dowse which properties might be interesting to you. Dowsing can even help you to determine the information that you most need before you make your decision to buy or build, although this will require that you think of appropriate questions.

A beginning question that you might want to use is, "All things considered, is this an appropriate piece of land for me to buy at this time?" Obviously, to use this wording you must have a conception of what "all things considered" means to you. It might mean within a certain distance from your work; the suitability of the land to your proposed use; whether it will meet certain requirements, including the needs of all family members; whether you want to make a home for animals or have a garden; whether the land is in your price range; and, very important, whether there is accessible good water and a way to deal with sewage without pollution to your, or anyone else's, water supply. As part of your spiritual quest, you might also wish to know whether there is some higher purpose connecting you to a particular spot. And you need to know whether this particular piece of land would welcome your intentions. You would want to dowse about the earth energies, especially whether there are any harmful water veins, other harmful earth energies, or psychic damage that would cause stress to those living on this property (remembering that you would be thinking of these factors from your present limited state of knowledge).

Water veins and other earth energies, both beneficial and harmful, will be described in chapters 11 and 12. Briefly, *psychic damage* means that some act of cruelty, physical or mental, has been committed on the land, which then holds the memory of that damage until it has been healed. As you will discover, something can be done, with the permissions received, to detoxify and harmonize many conditions. But you can ask now whether—if and when you were to become the custodian of the land—you would receive the necessary permissions.

Next you can dowse for positive energies on the land. These might include energy leys; if there are any on the property, honor them. (Don't plan to build a house over them but do designate as a meditation place any spot where such lines cross.) All this is dowsing you can do from home—as information dowsing or dowsing with a map of the property. When you do then see the land, you may dowse on-site to corroborate your findings. You will at least get a sense of the property and learn how you feel on different parts of it. It may at first surprise you that on-site your body "knows" something that you thought you had been learning through dowsing, and that you can also experience knowing by dowsing miles away from the site.

In our paradigm, changes may not be made on land without permission of the custodian, who is not you until you have "bought" the land. After you have done this, and if you have also received the other permissions, you can proceed to put everything to rights or to ask help from someone with more experience.

If you buy a particular piece of land, before you impose your will on it, it would be best to ask the land what its intention is regarding your being there. Where does the land want the house? Map-dowse or dowse on-site as you would to find a well site. Check the earth energies in regard to this spot. You may also want to ask for the location of any especially sacred spots on the land. Honor these places with your recognition as you begin to make contact with the invisible presences and with the animals and trees and plants on the land. All these are your helpers or are in your care and, if your intention is right, will be willing to cooperate with you to achieve harmony on the land.

You may become aware of devas and earth spirits as you dowse. Devas are of a different vibratory level than ours and represent the group souls of various animals, trees, plants, or minerals to whom they give direction. Earth spirits are also from a different vibratory level and appear to have a vital function as the usually invisible workers on the land.

If you plan to build a house, you may want to consider building with natural materials that do not have toxic side effects. Many aspects of dowsing lend themselves to the kinds of decisions needed to have a "natural house," increasingly important as we are assailed by more and more radiation and pollution. Dowsing can help you to make decisions about construction materials, insulation, the heating system, the lights, paints and stains, fabrics, and—once you've moved into the house—cleaning supplies. The importance of each choice depends on the people who will live in the house. Many people have allergies to common building materials; for them, decisions will be more critical than for those without allergies or with stronger immune systems. On a ten-point scale, you can dowse to decide the places where it is especially important to spend extra money for health's sake if you do not have enough funds to do everything in an ideal way.

To dowse on a ten-point scale, decide that ten means "most important," while one means "very little importance." As you count up or down, ask that your pendulum circle at the number that represents, in this case, the "actual importance" specific to a person at a particular time. You may use a ten-point scale for many kinds of questions so long as you first decide what the scale represents.

Color choices for walls, curtains, and furniture can be assisted through dowsing. Often what people like is what they need. Sometimes, however, particular colors, therapeutic in one situation, could be harmful in another.

As construction is done on the site, you will want to keep checking for negative entities, negative thought-forms, and any harmful changes in the earth-energy patterns so that, once the permissions are secured, any disharmonies may be set right. Negative entities are discarnate beings who have died but who cause harm by trying to "hang on" to this life instead of, as intended, moving on to their next proper place of development. Negative thought-forms are thoughts of a negative nature that, deliberately or inadvertently, may have been left behind by someone. Remember that thoughts are things and have life. If harmful thought-forms are found and we receive permission, we ask in prayer that these negative thought-forms be dissolved. We also try to be more aware of our own thoughts, attempting to keep them always positive.

Your intention in regard to the land is important. When finally you are ready to move into the house, a simple ceremony stating this intention is a good idea. No particular ceremony is required. The idea is to express the unity that you hope to achieve with the land and with the other inhabitants on it and to express your feeling that you will truly try to care for all to the best of your ability.

Decisions about the placements of gardens and plantings may be reached with dowsing. If you feel that certain trees and bushes are best removed, this may be checked through dowsing. (You might ask if it is to the highest good that this tree be removed at this time.) You may change your mind about your original intention as an alternative comes to mind. If a tree must come down and gives its permission for this through your dowsed response, the tree should have enough warning time to remove its life energy to a nearby tree of the same type. (Tell the tree mentally or out loud what you intend.) And when a tree must be cut, it should be done quickly and with respect.

For those who move into a house already built, many similar dowsing searches are applicable. We have already mentioned how to dowse prospective land, but you may also want to dowse the condition of the house—the state of the foundations, the location of damaged places that may be out of sight (as in a chimney).

Then there is cleanup. If you clean up and make beauty and order, you, the house, and the land will all visibly feel lightened and "breathe" relief. You will be able to see and feel the change.

In a not-new house you may also have all the remnants of other people's lives there, and you will want to set about correcting any disharmonies from the past and establishing your own contact with the land and with the house.

If you rent a house or an apartment, you are not the custodian; the owner is. In our paradigm, changes cannot be made in the subtle structure of the property without the owner's permission. But a request for protection from any disharmonies may be made on behalf of those living there. If these beings include attuned people, their presence alone may help toward the creation of harmony.

When buying new furniture, you can dowse its appropriateness for the intended use, its quality, and its sturdiness. You can do this from an advertisement before going to the store. If you buy used furniture or antiques, realize that these objects may have been psychically imprinted by those using them before. If we plan to buy something old, we have learned to dowse first to make sure that we are not bringing home anything with harmful imprints unless we also dowse that these disharmonies can be cleared through a simple prayer.

In our homes we have the opportunity to use color, pattern, and sound to help create harmony and beauty. You may find it useful to read books about feng shui (which will be described in chapter 11) and radionics (see the David Tansley titles in the recommended readings) to understand a little of what pattern may mean. You may also want to dowse in connection with the music that you introduce into your home and so learn what sounds and frequencies are conducive to harmony and well-being. Your study might include reading about extremely low frequencies (ELF frequencies) that, although below our conscious level of hearing, have profound effect upon us. (For more information see the books by Dr. Robert O. Becker listed in the recommended readings.)

On a day-to-day basis, the color of clothing we choose to wear affects us, for it's as though we are giving ourselves a bath in these colors. Some dowsers do indeed give light baths, using colored gels, either to themselves or for dowsed periods of time to photographs. (The photograph provides a focus.) Not only the color but the fabric of our clothing is significant, for many people have allergies to synthetic fabrics. Our clothing choices may also need to reflect the way we feel about uses of the environment and of other beings. Again, dowsing can help us to gain the information with which to make intelligent decisions.

You may also dowse for food. One way to practice is to have someone put an item in each of several paper bags. One might be a food you like that is good for you, another something that doesn't agree with you, yet another an inedible cleaning product. Dowse which bags have in them items safe and good for you to eat. Open the bags for instant feedback.

You may check your results with kinesiology. A simple kinesiology test is to have the person being tested stand in front of you with the left arm outstretched, the other relaxed at the side. Facing the person, put your left hand on his or her right shoulder and, with your right hand just above his or her wrist, push down on the extended arm. Note the degree of strength in the arm. Next, in the relaxed hand put one of the bags mentioned above. Again push down on the extended arm. Is the person weaker than before, stronger than before, the same? This is not a foolproof test (various factors can affect it), but it is an interesting way to show that your body knows a lot about what items might be good for you (a stronger reaction), are okay (the same), or are harmful to you (a weaker reaction).

At the supermarket, dowse on a ten-point scale (ten being highest), all things considered, how good are these carrots? Do they contain harmful chemicals (yes or no)? Is the vitamin level low after long storage? When will this avocado be fully ripe? (Tomorrow? Three days from now?) Perhaps you decide to buy a bottle of wine. Price does not tell it all; dowse its quality on a ten-point scale, ten being the best possible. (Remember to start counting with the pendulum in search position, with the understanding that as you get to the correct answer the pendulum will circle.) Eight on a ten-point scale? Pretty good; that's one to buy. Ask what you need to know, remembering to frame the questions in yes or no form.

Vitamins can be dowsed in a similar way, and it is a good idea to dowse daily since our supplement needs are not always the same. Would it be to my best interest to take some more vitamin C today? Yes. Less than 500 milligrams? No. More than 1000 milligrams? No. 750 milligrams? Yes.

When you go out to a restaurant, dowse what choice on the menu is best for you at this time. To choose a restaurant in a strange city, friends of ours dowse using sound as their "tool," by saying "Om" as they drive by an unknown restaurant. When the sound is full and clear, that means that it's a good restaurant. If the sound is not clear, they drive on until they find a restaurant that gets a "yes" response. Of course, you can use conventional dowsing tools instead of sound to choose a restaurant.

In regard to health and healing there are many ways that dowsing can be of great assistance. Certainly making healthful choices regarding our homes, our food, and our clothing is important. And even if you don't yet feel that you are able to do what is needed to detoxify a noxious water vein, you can learn to find one and move a bed or a favorite chair away from it (noxious water veins are discussed in chapters 11 and 12). You can learn to ask whether your bed is facing in the optimum direction for you at this time. If not, in which direction should it face? Walk around with your rods or pendulum until you get "yes" to a position. You can dowse how many hours of sleep per night are best for you. Do you think you might have an allergy? With dowsing you can ask questions that will help you tell your doctor what you think might need to be checked.

When you need medical help, you can dowse whether an allopathic, homeopathic, osteopathic, or chiropractic physician, or someone else would be most helpful. If you are in a strange town and need a doctor and there is no medical association to ask, you can dowse down the list in the phone book and find the best available help.

Is this a situation in which flower remedies would help? Herbal medicine? Vitamins? Specific foods? Is there something else that needs to be asked at this time?

This last question is a very important one, for if the answer is yes, then the present thinking about a situation is not sufficient and we must keep trying to find out what more we need to know and so to ask.

Please note that in none of these health matters are we

suggesting that traditional medical aid should not be sought. What dowsing and prayer can do is apart from that realm, and it is ethically very important that a dowser not give any kind of well-meaning advice that could inadvertently result in harm. In many states, dowsers are not allowed by law to diagnose for other people, but diagnosis is not necessary for the healing prayer described in chapter 13. We want to be able to stay within the guidelines of the law in what we do and teach.

Of course, for ourselves, we are free to try to diagnose what is wrong, just for the interest of it. A doctor's diagnosis is also often based on intuition, as many doctors have written, but a doctor also has the information to allow differentiation among a variety of possibilities of which we might not even be aware.

There are endless ways in which dowsing can contribute to our health and to our peace of mind. Going on vacation? Which proposed route would be most harmonious? How is the water in the vacation cabin? Safe to drink? Need to buy bottled water? Which of these six brands of bottled water is the best, dowsed on a ten-point scale? A family member is not yet home. Is the person safe? Held up in traffic? Is my car safe for driving? No. Is the problem in the motor? No. Brakes? Yes. Is the brake fluid low? Yes. Is that the only problem? Yes. With more brake fluid, will the car then be safe for driving? Yes. Away from home, the car needs attention. Which garage is best to call? With a finger moving down the list in the local phone book, ask that your pendulum circle when you come to the garage that will best help with this particular problem.

Where did I leave the car keys? In the car? In the kitchen?

I have lost my watch and I was in ten stores today. Is it now in any of them? Yes. Start naming them, asking that your pendulum circle when you locate the right one. Then go to that store's lost-and-found and see if you can reclaim the watch.

Which rose bush at the nursery will do best in our yard? Use an L-rod and ask that it point toward that plant. Once home with it, ask to be shown the optimum place to plant it. Do this by turning in a circle, holding an L-rod in search position. As you turn, the rod should soon stay pointing in the appropriate direction. Triangulate. Walk to the spot indicated and ask that the rod spin (or the pendulum circle) over the exact spot. In which direction should the plant face? Turn the pot until your dowsing tool indicates "yes, that's it."

You can see that dowsing has many uses in everyday matters but that some questions may be more important to answer correctly than others. You don't want to wait until you desperately need an answer before you begin to practice, which is why we suggest that you dowse every day and begin with things you can easily verify.

In dowsing, one receives subtle instruction in refining the question. For example, one might check before making a long-distance station-to-station call that the person one wishes to speak with is at that number.

One might dowse the question, "Is John home?"

On one occasion we asked this about someone and got yes, but when we made the call we were told that the person was not there but was "home"—visiting family in another state. We were thus taught to be more precise in the question asked.

"Now" or another specific time is something else that is often important to add to the dowsing question, since we are not limited in our searches to present time. One might also wish to ask, when dowsing before phoning, "Is this person able to speak with me now?" since it is possible that he or she might be in the shower.

Here are some more possibilities for quick verification of your dowsing. What time will the mail be delivered today? Before 2:00 P.M.? Yes. Before 1:00 P.M.? No. Before 1:30? Yes.

Keep asking yes and no questions to narrow down the time until you arrive at a precise figure, the same way you do when you ask for the depth of a water vein. When the mail is delivered, you will see whether or not you were correct.

What is the amount of the phone bill just received but still in the envelope? Ask yes and no questions in this same manner until you come up with a figure. Then open the envelope and see if you were right.

Now, what if you are wrong? This is not the time to decide that you will never dowse again. You are being given a valuable lesson. Does this involve re-forming the question to lessen ambiguity, or did your rational mind get in the way? Did you think, the mailman always gets here at 1:00 P.M. and "dowse" that and instead he came at 1:25? If this happened, did you have a little feeling at the same time that you were getting that answer that maybe it wasn't right? Start watching those little feelings. Note when you feel that some answer "must" be correct because your rational self "says" it is. Sometimes after asking a question and getting a response, it is useful to ask, as we learned from Reshad Feild, "Is this the truth?" If you get "no," then start your questions over again.

Do you know enough about what you're looking for to be clear? Beginners frequently confuse energy leys and water because they are not really sure about the nature of each. If this happens, you need to know more about these targets and, if possible, to go out and dowse beside a competent dowser who can set you straight.

Jack Livingston, one of the greatest American dowsers, was always much more interested in his mistakes than in his thousands of successes, because, as he said, it is from your mistakes that you can learn something new. Everyone makes mistakes, but some learn from them and some do not. Don't gloss over a mistake. Admit it, and then find out what it has to teach you.

A beginning dowser would be wise to check his or her yes and no responses regularly; for some people these occasionally reverse. If you find that this happens, here are a couple of suggestions. One is to tap a few times lightly on your thymus area; this idea comes from Dr. John Diamond's book about kinesiology, *The Body Doesn't Lie*. Another suggestion is to put your tongue on the little button behind your front teeth, as is done in some meditations. This appears to have a balancing effect, and beginners seem to get clearer yes and no responses after doing this. Remember to ask the permissions. If the "Can I?" receives a "no," you might be too tired to get correct answers at this time. Learning to dowse is exciting and at first very tiring, because we are beginning to train ourselves in a way that has been neglected in our society. Of course you are tired. Rest and try again later.

We have mentioned the value of keeping a daily dowsing journal. This will help you to remember what you have learned and will often provide valuable clues to questions that may arise in the future. And you will have a record of your progress.

Dowsing can be used in so many ways, and you will find it interesting to think of new ones. An example of an unusual use is the fascinating account of a dowsing search into past history recorded in Jan de Hartog's novel *The Centurion*; in it he describes in fictional terms his own dowsing pursuit that became the book. As part of this search he map-dowsed where he should go to discover pieces of the story; one location he didn't at first understand was where he discovered a streambed that revealed remnants of a Roman road. At each stage of his dowsing-led journey, Jan de Hartog (and the dowsing character in his book) asked a series of questions that elicited information.

The Centurion beautifully illustrates the process of one question leading to the next. When you begin, questions often don't come easily. You have to work hard to think of what they should be. But as you dowse more and more, often a question will just swim into consciousness that, when answered, will give you the next piece of information you need. This is one of the most exciting aspects of learning to dowse.

You will find your daily dowsing increasingly useful if you give it continued, attentive practice. Sometimes, however, people use dowsing to ask direction for every single thing they do in their lives. This, we feel, is not dowsing's intended function. It is our responsibility to make decisions, although dowsing can help to give us the information from which to make good ones.

How can you use dowsing right now to help in your spiritual unfoldment? At every stage you can dowse to evaluate what might be a practical and appropriate next step. In looking over a book list, is there a book here that I need at this time? Standing in a bookshop or in a library, ask, is there a book here that "speaks" to me at this time? On which shelf? Point, or look and dowse. Or draw a floor plan of the library or bookstore and map-dowse from home. When information on a so-called spiritual workshop comes in the mail, dowse on a ten-point scale its value to you now—or, better, its value when the workshop is to take place (they might not be the same response). And, in the same way, you can dowse the appropriateness of any potential teacher for you at this time.

Remember also that these practical uses are not merely ends-in-themselves but serve as means of refining the dowsing skill for more advanced applications when you are ready.

And now, after this brief overview of the early stages of dowsing, we move on to a way of thinking that we feel is an appropriate framework for the further stages.

PART TWO

PARADIGM: A WAY OF THINKING

✳

*Spiritual progress comes
by changing one's point of view.2*

—*Pir Vilayat Inayat Khan*

5

THE SEA OF MIND

We are particularly interested in the interface of dowsing, consciousness, and spirituality. We understand the expansion of spirituality to correspond to the expansion of consciousness, and we suggest that the most advanced stages of dowsing are not so much what one learns to do as what one learns to *be*. Ultimately that means the recognition of our total dependence on God for everything and the realization that only as God moves through us are we able to be catalysts for any of those changes that we understand to be for the highest good. Asking always that what we do be in harmony with God's will for the highest good—"Thy will be done"—is, we feel, the appropriate frame of mind for the dowser hoping to be of service by working in the fifth and sixth levels of dowsing. At the seventh level, if ever in that state, the dowser would for that time cease to be an individual self and be resonant with the Creative Will of the universe, the Mind of God.

As we unfold our dowsing capabilities within the seven-stage paradigm, we gradually move from using our lens systems of perception to using a holographic system. When we are conscious of these two systems of awareness and of the many levels within our dowsing, we can then choose among them the most appropriate for a particular situation. Physicist David Bohm and physiologist Karl Pribram both indicate that the actual structure, function, and activity of thought is in the implicate order, and one of our goals as we unfold the stages of dowsing is to be able to reach, with increasingly subtle levels of awareness, those aspects of our being that *already exist* at those more subtle, formative levels.

When we work solely within a lenslike system, we can bring only one aspect of a problem or situation into focus at a time. If we are not careful, that one aspect may develop as a "groove" in our thinking, so that our understanding becomes limited by this narrowed perspective of our consciousness. (This would be like a person deciding to improve health by focusing entirely on diet, to the exclusion of all other factors.)

One way we can move beyond grooves of the mind and increase the scope of our consciousness is to learn to meditate. Regular meditation practice allows consciousness to function more harmoniously at all levels, including those beyond the lenslike systems of thought.

David Bohm has indicated that a person's mind will tend to operate according to the way that person thinks. If external reality is thought of as composed of separate items, then both thought and action will be fragmented. If it is thought of as part of an undivided, harmonious whole, then the mind will move in a similar way to suggest actions that flow in an orderly manner from that concept.[3] The more we can develop this kind of truly holistic awareness, the better we will be able to understand what are appropriate requests and actions within a given context. While we are learning to do this, we can prevent a great deal of harmful action by always remembering and correctly dowsing the permission questions—May I? Can I? Should I?

We use the paradigm of the seven stages of dowsing as a framework to allow us to understand that there are levels of unfoldment in the dowsing journey. No dowser ever needs to feel required to progress through all seven stages, and much good and useful service may be done by a stage-one dowser, but what it is important to realize, even if one chooses not to go further, is that there is always more to learn.

In our attempts to define our lives we are accustomed to spinning mental cocoons around ourselves, cocoons that become increasingly snug and comfortable. In fact, we tend to feel threatened when anything impinges upon us from outside these cocoons. If left unexamined, conditioning is easily thought to be "truth," and anything outside the cocoon as "not the truth."

For most people, dowsing is outside the cocoon; and even some dowsers feel uncomfortable about the idea of advanced stages of dowsing.

We may have the best of intentions, but it is still difficult to break through our own cocoons, even when we need to do so. At each stage we need to reexamine assumptions and to remember that no matter how advanced we may think we are, we can still create closed systems and convince ourselves, erroneously, that our development is complete.

We can avoid this error if we remember that each of us is a fraction of the universe but that at the same time we are linked on subtle levels to all other fractions of the universe. These subtle connections are established by what we call resonance, not just on a gross level but on finer and finer levels. When we reach the finest level, we then "are" also the totality, which means that every cell of our bodies thus contains in essence the code for the entire universe.

If this progression is indeed true, then our thinking, or our consciousness, is also part of the continual unfolding through the implicate to the explicate order. Because our everyday reality, including our thinking, emerges originally from undifferentiated wholeness, it follows that everything is permeated with this subtle aspect of consciousness. That is why we can think of our own minds as localized islands of consciousness in this sea of mind. Existing as separate bits of apparent reality, we are the ones who unknowingly put barriers around these islands of consciousness. Even so, we are still surrounded by, and are a part of, the unbounded sea of mind that we may experience to the degree that we are willing to learn to remove barriers. That is what we begin to do when we learn to dowse.

Itzhak Bentov has said that each individual human consciousness is part of the hologram he calls the Universal Mind and that, by extending individual consciousness, knowledge about the whole universe may be obtained.[4] Furthermore, David Bohm's theory, with its consideration of a state of primary unity, implies to us that the person dowsing knows the answer to a question before it is even asked. In order to realize this, however, we go through the ritual of asking the question and getting a response before we can become aware of the answer. When we learn to dowse, we create this ritual by using a dowsing tool to open our awareness beyond what we call objective reality, so that the information we are seeking may then unfold.

In the more advanced stages of dowsing we must be willing to extend our awareness to deeper levels of subtlety within, as well as outside of, ourselves. We may then discover—and experience—the surrounding world as a mirror for everything within, and everything within as a mirror for everything that lies outside. Someone at this stage of awareness is no longer interacting with surroundings but *is* these surroundings at an essential level of reality. When the dowser's consciousness allows this degree of realization, then this person's dowsing may become reflexive to the basic impulses governing the trembling of leaves and the movement of stars.

One difficulty, however, is that the advanced levels on the path cannot really be understood by the terminology or assumptions of the earlier levels. As a result, people sometimes confuse levels and undertake activities inappropriate for a particular stage. You thus find people, for example, attempting to "heal" without being aware of the subtle, resonant levels of responsibility inherent in the process. All activities ultimately have universal significance, but until we realize this directly, it is just so many words.

Remember that the levels of progression in dowsing are also levels of attunement. This does not mean that a dowser able to function on the sixth level of dowsing is no longer able to do on-site water dowsing. It does mean that such a dowser will be able to bring to on-site water dowsing awareness learned through the unfoldment of skill in the advanced stages. To the viewer, however, the dowser may still appear merely to "chop wood and carry water."

6

CONSCIOUSNESS

When you first learn to dowse, you are naturally delighted that the tool moves in response to a target or a question. Years ago one of our students was especially excited when he discovered that by dowsing he could find both true north and magnetic north. For several days he took the time to check these out and each time he smiled and nodded. He knew that there were other things he could do with dowsing, but for a little while he simply wanted to play at dowsing and to enjoy finding north. Obviously, if that student had viewed dowsing as consisting solely of looking for north, his idea of dowsing would have been limited. Not so obviously, if a person thinks of dowsing solely in terms of looking for water or minerals, his or her idea of dowsing is likewise limited.

Many dowsers reach a certain level or stage of competence in dowsing and decide to stay there. If they have consciously made that choice but are still pleased to hear what other dowsers are up to, at least they recognize that there is more to dowsing than a particular aspect or level of it that they have chosen. If they teach others to dowse, then, when their students learn all that they are able to teach, they can refer those students to teachers more appropriate for further stages.

As we master each progressive stage of dowsing, we also need to recognize and accept an increasing degree of inherent responsibility, just as we need to do in each progressive stage of spiritual unfoldment. While it is true that we feel delight and wonder at every advancement in dowsing and spiritual unfoldment, those wonderful feelings may tempt the dowser or seeker to remain at that stage. Every step in the personal journey contains a spiritual challenge to move still further, but, if that challenge is not recognized, the psychic side effects of that step—what Reshad Feild calls "the world of attraction"—may eclipse the dowser's awareness of the challenge.

Joseph Chilton Pearce spoke of the confusion between the psychic and the spiritual when he explained that "there is a sharp quantum break between psychic and spiritual, and you can add all psychic phenomena up from here to eternity and it will never give you one tiny iota of a step toward the spiritual." He did not intend his comment to denigrate the psychic, however. He also said:

> The psychic is one of our tools; it's one of our playthings. It opens up a whole realm of activity which is legitimate, but never mistake the psychic for the spiritual. The spiritual generates from one place, the heart, and it has nothing to do with anything but that relational energy which ties everything into its absolute unity.[5]

The psychic is a plaything. If you choose a spiritual path, enjoy the playthings, but also keep in mind that the plaything is at best a temporary interruption from the discipline of the path.

If beginning dowsers accept a system or paradigm that allows them to evaluate their evolving levels of skill and use permissions as checks and balances along the way, these will guide them through the unfolding of increasingly subtle stages of attunement or resonance. We may use the term *resonance* in regard to shortwave receivers and electronic direction finders, but another way to understand it is to think of striking a note on a musical instrument when there is another similar musical instrument in the same area. The second instrument will produce a similar sound or a harmonic of the original sound—one kind of resonance. Now think of a shortwave receiver as another kind of instrument, this time responding to a higher (or more subtle) frequency of vibration. It can be placed in an area more distant from the source, even in a different part of the world. One could still affect the other, this time at another level of resonance.

The process of dowsing depends on resonance. The mental image you form allows this resonance to occur between your image and the target in a way appropriate to your level of dowsing activity. As a result of specific resonance, the dowser then translates vibratory patterns into an answer appropriate to the dowsing question and to the stage at which he or she is working.

Most people can understand the concept of resonance, but they may still have trouble relating it to dowsing. If so, they may find it helpful to relate the concept to the idea of the explicate order, the realm of everyday reality with which we are immediately familiar in our daily lives because it has to do with everything experienced through our senses. The implicate order could be understood to be like those frequencies of energy that create resonance through an antenna and are then decoded into another "order" of energy: sound or image. The implicate order, however—the realm of primary reality—is of a vastly different order of energy from that of radio signals. This energy is not dependent on a position in space but is present everywhere. The resonance unfolded from it is much more subtle but also much more powerful than that created in the explicate order. All of our everyday reality is unfolded from these patterns created in the implicate order, as a three-dimensional holographic image is unfolded from the seemingly random two-dimensional wave patterns spread over a photographic plate. These wave patterns of the implicate order are also enfolded in turn with even more subtlety into an underlying state of Unity, from which all of creation unfolds at the appropriate time and in the appropriate place. It is somewhat similar to what mystics speak of when they refer to this world of multiplicity as being but a fragmented reflection of a single, powerful Unity—like different colored shards of glass reflecting the light of a single sun.

From this point of view, we are a fraction of the universe, but at the same time we are also linked by subtle strands with all other fragments, and this link is established by resonance. In other words, each fraction not only vibrates of its own accord but it echoes or re-creates the sound of vibrations from all other fragments. If you advance your skill to the fifth or sixth stages, you begin to gain access to those subtle strands and at the same time to have an effect on them whether you want to do so or not. And the more subtle we become in our awareness or in our dowsing, the more completely we can discover the interrelatedness—the interdependence—of all things. According to Bell's theorem, if you have two electrons in harmonious vibration, even though they may be a universe apart, whenever you change the spin of one the other simultaneously will change its spin too. By the seventh stage of dowsing, when the dowser may touch upon the harmony of all created matter, thought and action reflexively affect everything else.

We can gain even more insight into this term *resonance* in the context of the theory of formative causation developed by British biologist Rupert Sheldrake. He suggests that morphogenetic fields act as blueprints for known phenomena. These fields, called M-fields, work across both time and space, and living things throughout their life cycles "tune in" to the appropriate sequence of M-fields through a process of "morphic resonance." The resonance causes these forms to be maintained and repeated, giving rise to the regularities—habits—of nature. In addition, this concept of fields of vibration causing resonance allows for the possibility of revision at appropriate levels of formation or causation whenever factors outside that level are revised.[6] In other words, at every stage of our being we are in essence involved actively in multidirectional, multidimensional processes—whether we intend to be or not.

Now the question is, does all this really relate to dowsing, and even if it does, what does it have to do with spiritual unfoldment? Is ours an appropriate paradigm? Let's look at some things that suggest that we may be on the right track.

In the early 1980s a psychiatrist, Edith Jurka, did a series of tests using a Mind Mirror (a version of an electroencephalograph) to look at brain-wave patterns of dowsers.[7] She discovered that those brain-wave patterns studied were similar to ones produced by experienced meditators and sometimes corresponded with those described for mystics. Although these patterns were more prominent in long-term dowsers, they were also present to some degree in relative newcomers; and some of the experienced dowsers showed patterns that indicated a level of attunement corresponding to what had been associated with "cosmic consciousness." These tests, along with anecdotal evidence from advanced dowsers, suggest that, like the mystic, the dowser is attuned to increasingly subtle levels of reality. Unlike the mystic, however, the dowser may be so attuned whether he or she consciously tries to be or not—and, more noteworthy, whether or not the resposibilities inherent to that attunement are recognized. Some experienced dowsers appeared to show brain patterns indicative of a search whether or not they were dowsing; in other words, for experienced dowsers that brain pattern would seem to have become part of their natural state.

We realize, of course, that an EEG readout is merely an external indication of electrical impulses from the brain—a side effect, if you will, of some sort of activity that is really beyond our comprehension. The organizing fields maintaining the pattern, as well as brain activity for even a simple task, are tremendously complex; every one of the neurons is in potential resonance with all fields of enfolded subtle energy throughout the universe. When we go down to the level of the DNA and those forces that give shape to the DNA, we find that this subtle but profound coding in each cell of each individual is in potential resonance with the essential coding of all of creation.

If you think of resonance as a multidirectional process, you may see what sort of responsibility this creates in your dowsing: you are not only picking up various signals from a concrete or abstract target by resonance, but you are also affecting the target itself, as well as all similar targets. The degree to which you affect the target is directly proportional to the stage from which you are dowsing, which means that the further you advance, the greater becomes your degree of responsibility.

When taught to dowse by an experienced teacher, a beginner is told repeatedly that the answers received are determined by the content of the questions asked. This also means that the frame of thought within which a question is asked determines the frame of the answer received. Although dowsing is primarily an intuitive affair, relying heavily on the "right brain," this is the stage—the framing of the question—at which the role of the "left brain" becomes critically important. The more we know about that which we are seeking, the sharper and more cogent our questions will be. Since dowsing appears to be surprisingly literal, at least in the learning stages, knowledge becomes critical.

As with a shortwave receiver, we may also tune ourselves to various signals and receive appropriate responses, but we must learn to discriminate, just as a receiver discriminates among stations. Without discrimination we are like a receiver operating on too wide a receiving band. With discrimination we can make our reception more and more refined and increase our sensitivity in a way analogous to that between a one-transistor toy radio and a multiband receiver with tens of thousands of miniaturized printed circuits.

As you learn to fine-tune your capacity to receive information, so too can you learn to put it into wider and wider context—as when you climb a mountain, each stage at which you look down shows a larger view. During our spiritual journey, if we review our own lives from the perspective of our journey up the mountain, we can better understand that limitations of our mind-sets determined how we processed information at each earlier stage, both as to what we included and what we excluded.

The more we become able to understand the nature of the object or of the information sought, the more resonant will we be to its more subtle aspects. When moving to more subtle stages of consciousness through dowsing, we also change the way we process information.

At each stage of personal transformation our awareness of the cosmos expands and we realize more fully the magnitude and subtlety of the world around us. We then discover the mirror image of this expanded cosmos that lies within each one of us. Once we break through our own limitations enough to see that the inner and outer aspects of our being mirror each other, we can turn inward to our own hearts to realize the Oneness—the Unity—present at the heart of all existence. We can then bring this awareness back to everyday life.

7

MEDITATION

During our journey from childhood to adulthood we develop habitual responses to the world around us and conditioned patterns of thought about the nature of that world. Only rarely do we develop the skills needed to break away from those patterns. One good way to free yourself from them is through meditation. Meditation allows us to extend the limits of our perception and expand our awareness both of ourselves and of the world around us. We recommend that you use the tool of meditation to move toward the stillness and centeredness that are essential to the advanced dowser. If you practice regularly over a period of time, you will discover that as you increase proficiency in the ability to meditate, you also increase the effectiveness and range of your dowsing.

Meditation is conventionally thought of as any one of a variety of techniques used to still the mind and body into a state of harmony. When we approach that state, our presumptions of separation between mind and body begin to dissolve, and these two aspects of self start to merge into one integrated whole. One might think of it as mind and body becoming extensions of each other. This perception of wholeness then helps to create a capacity for more subtle levels of awareness, beyond those customarily limited to rational mind and physical body.

Many factors are a part of the process that leads to a sense of unity: hemispheric activities and revised neural connections in the cortex, release of biochemicals in the midbrain, revisions of brain-wave patterns (as would show up on an EEG), and changes in the flow of subtle energies. When all these observable factors harmonize during meditation, they produce even more subtle effects that continue beyond the period of meditation.

Consciously or unconsciously, most dowsers desire this state of unity for a very simple reason: they can dowse better when they are in that state. They may not realize, however, that their progress toward that state began with their first use of a dowsing tool. When we first learn to dowse we think in terms of self and instrument. That thought frees us from the assumption that our mind is creating a bodily reaction or that one hemisphere of the brain is dominating the other hemisphere. As a result, we act as though the instrument is producing the response. This indirection permits separate aspects of the brain to have a greater natural capacity to work in balance. Acting as though the response comes from the instrument allows beginners to remain objective as they become accustomed to receiving verifiable responses. Later on they can become more aware that their accuracy corresponds directly to some degree of inner harmony.

This state of harmony is analogous to the state reached during meditation, when activities of the brain are stilled and its hemispheres become more closely balanced. Those who dowse regularly find that their ability to meditate is enhanced, and those who meditate regularly likewise discover that their capacity to dowse increases.

Meditation has no simple definition because, like dowsing, it is a process, and the techniques used depend on your stage of development and on the reason for the meditation. These reasons can range from the superficial, such as a desire for a few moments of stillness, to the more profound, such as a yearning for a sense of unity with all of creation. Within some mystical traditions, meditation allows students to develop their concentration to such an extent that every moment of life may be lived in a state of heightened awareness. Working, resting, conversing—all become aspects of one's meditation. No matter what techniques are used, all meditations have one preliminary goal: to lead the student to an inner center of stillness.

Here are a few simple practices that will help you to develop both concentration and inner balance.

To begin, find a comfortable place to sit where you will not be disturbed or interrupted. You may choose a straight-backed chair on which you can sit with both feet on the floor, or a cushion on which you can sit cross-legged. You should be able to keep your back straight without muscle tension. You might imagine that a taut cord, held from above, passes up your spine and through the top of your head.

Next, close your eyes and give your attention to your breath. At first act as though you are merely an observer, noticing the inbreath and the outbreath. Then you slowly allow the breath to become centered in the diaphragm—you can feel the movement if you place your palm there. Your breathing should be slow and full without being forced. If you need to take a deep breath, go ahead and do so, but then return to regular diaphragm breathing.

You now balance your inbreath and outbreath, both in capacity and in duration. Think of the two breaths like the slow, steady swing of a pendulum. If the effort to keep your breath balanced creates tension, try breathing even more slowly and regularly. The degree of impersonal attention you can give to the breath makes a difference, but you can still take an occasional deep breath if you need to do so.

You will notice that as you give your breath more attention, you begin to perceive your heartbeat. If you wish, you can breathe in rhythm with it. This will make it easier to maintain the balance of the breath.

That's all there is to the first practice, but you will find that it does take a while to master. You will also find it most helpful if you can practice it with full attention at a regular time each day.

In the next stage, you observe closely the nature of the breath. Follow the same initial preparation that you did in the first practice and then balance your breathing. This time give your attention to the air as it first enters the nostrils. Perceive it closely, as if someone had asked you to identify a very subtle fragrance. Observe the obvious qualities of the air, such as temperature, moisture, various odors, and then try to note the less obvious characteristics, such as the presence of dust and the nature of the gases in the atmosphere. If you find yourself growing tense, simply allow that tension to flow down through the spine and out of your body as you breathe out.

When you feel that there is no more to discover about the air as it enters your nose, next observe its quality as it passes through your sinuses. Again, you first observe the obvious qualities, both of the inbreath and of the outbreath, and then the more subtle qualities. Be sure to remain relaxed. At first you may feel light-headed, but that feeling will pass if you breathe more slowly and with greater attention.

You then follow the breath down the back of the throat and note the characteristics of the air as it passes downward and returns upward. Your attention to your breath will become even more refined and subtle as you slowly relax your throat muscles.

Finally—and this requires the most practice—you note the condition of the air as it passes into the lungs, reaches the capillaries, and begins its exchange with the blood. You will be able to verify this exchange indirectly as you sense the increased energy that results from the enriched blood in your system. You may even be able to follow the flow of the blood through each part of the body. If you are able to give attention to the exchange of subtle energies carried by the breath, you will correspondingly experience even more greatly this increase of energy throughout the body.

This process of following the breath allows you to "tune in" to your whole body. It has a particular advantage directly related to your dowsing ability in that it helps you to learn to focus your attention on a nonverbal, nonrational process.

As you master these preliminary stages of meditation, remember that they are also preparation for further stages, just as mastery of each stage of dowsing is also preparation for the next stage. You may practice them every day, but remember to keep the process gentle and to feel free to vary the breathing as required.

We recommend that you practice meditation with the same degree of attention that you would give to developing good dowsing practices. When you dowse, you focus on doing work "out there," even though you create an analog of that work within yourself; with meditation you concentrate on the work within, realizing that it also has its external analog. The two are connected, whether we want them to be or not, and one of our goals is to allow the connection to develop harmoniously.

After you have become familiar with the first two meditation practices, you can add one more element.

Begin by once more sitting upright, centering the breath in the solar plexus, and balancing the inbreath with the outbreath. Then you observe the flow of air through the nose, sinuses, esophagus, and lungs—until you feel the corresponding flow of energy through your body. Now give your attention to the rhythmic motion of the solar plexus. Notice its movement, like that of a pendulum, and let it proceed so that there is no jarring as your breath changes direction; let the changes occur easily in a continuous, smooth cycle.

Observe this motion back and forth and then imagine that, as with a pendulum, it is motion at the end of a cord suspended from above. Just as you may trace the movement of a pendulum upward along the cord toward the fingers that hold it with virtually no motion, you may similarly follow the breath inward until, with its increasing subtlety of motion, it reaches that point from which motion originates.

As we breathe in balance and follow the increasing subtlety of our breath as it takes us more deeply within, we are not only breathing in the gaseous substance of the air, but we are also involved in an exchange of subtle levels of energy that lie within the fabric of the air. Eventually, as we approach the still center from which the breath originates, we reach the level that extends beyond the outward show of energy and we approach the realm of pure spirit existing within us at the heart of all motion. The air we are breathing flows into us and out of us like a subtle counterpart of water. We may now allow our awareness to dissolve until we are at rest in that center, even though we are surrounded by motion. We remain there, both participant and observer, until we know it is time to return. This is the stillness that we then carry in our memory as we return slowly to our everyday condition.

The final stage of this meditation is one that you will discover by yourself. It comes not by will but as a beneficence. It follows the first three stages and emerges occasionally when you respond in harmony with the meditation practices. It will be centered in the fourth chakra, the subtle heart. When you reach it, for one timeless moment you are offered a glimpse not of the point of stillness but of the Source of that point of stillness.

After you have experienced the stillness at the center of

your *own* being, you will then learn to perceive the stillness at the heart of everything outside your own self. Then you will begin to sense and resonate with the fabric of interconnectedness joining all those essential forces of matter.

As you practice the full range of this meditation, the balance that you are able to create within yourself will subtly but significantly affect your ability to dowse. The effects will begin to occur as you reach the stage at which your mind and body merge into a larger concept of wholeness on both the conscious and unconscious levels. There the rational process you learned from childhood becomes balanced with the intuitive.

These practices do require deep but effortless concentration, and it is this delicately focused concentration that carries over into dowsing. When you master the middle stages of dowsing, your need for an external dowsing tool fades. It is as if the mind and the body, the intuitive and the rational, become a single dowsing instrument, thereby allowing you to become attuned to those increasingly subtle levels of the dowsing spectrum.

Our concern in meditation is not with kinds of energies or noxious forces or auras or any of those other specifics. Our intent is to develop balanced awareness so that we may remain in harmony with ourselves and our environment at every stage of the dowsing journey.

PART THREE

COOPERATION WITH NATURE: STAGE FIVE

✳

*A human being is a part of the whole, called by us
the "universe," a part limited in time and space. He
experiences himself, his thoughts and feelings, as
something separated from the rest—a kind of optical
delusion of his consciousness. This delusion is a kind
of prison for us, restricting us to our personal desires
and to affection for a few persons nearest to us. Our
task must be to free ourselves from this prison by
widening our circle of compassion to embrace all
living creatures and the whole of nature in its
beauty.[8]*

—Albert Einstein

*With an attitude, a specific intent and a moment of
concentrated communication with the subtle forms of
nature, all the forces of the universe will be focused
on bringing about the results.[9]*

—T. Edward Ross 2nd

8

PLANETARY CONSCIOUSNESS

The final stage in each cycle of personal transformation is to bring back to everyday life what we have learned. Our responsibility is then not only to the physical being of our planet but also to all the orders and kingdoms of beings that inhabit this globe. As we allow our awareness to grow, and as we deepen our capacity to perceive connections with all levels and forms of creation, we also increase our ability to become more effective stewards of our planetary home.

As we progress on our journeys, our view will gradually widen, as happened for astronaut Russell Schweikert, who circled the earth, looked down, was aware of all the wars and disputes going on just as they were before he left, but saw that there were no lines dividing countries. He saw instead in one grand view the ground upon which all of humankind's great art and philosophy were nurtured. Astronaut Edgar Mitchell saw the entire planet as a precious jewel shining in the darkness, a jewel to cherish and preserve.

As we become more aware of crises in the world, we remember that crisis is also opportunity. In our own journeys we can learn to develop the mountaintop or the space-capsule perspective, one that is part of an open rather than a closed system. We can learn to understand crises not only in their immediate impact but as part of a larger and evolving pattern.

Not only as dowsers but as spiritual seekers wishing to play an active part toward the resolution of planetary crises, we must discover for ourselves the extent to which we are locked within our own closed systems. We know that one problem in attempting to create an open-ended belief system is that our brains act as filters, with over 90 percent of the perceptual information available to us being filtered out. Much of this detuning, or shutting out, is necessary for sanity and takes place reflexively, but some of it happens as a result of conscious choice.

Many scientists still operate from closed systems, and their presuppositions determine the kinds of theories and experiments that they then formulate. A consequence of a self-replicating and self-justifying system is that only those theories and claims that follow its rules and presuppositions are brought forth within it. "Troublesome" observations are often dismissed as "epiphenomenal," a label used to invalidate or make irrelevant phenomena worthy of investigation but outside the closed system.

Classic physics describes a mechanistic order subject to immutable laws. That view works splendidly within the system that it defines but it cannot easily be adapted to fit new facts, such as the "new" fact that the universe now appears more accurately described as a web of relationships and habits. We need to reawaken our awareness of our own connection with and participation in a living world in which we do not stand alone.

The idea of interconnectedness is paradoxical to our conventional way of thinking. We customarily have assumed a superior stance in relation to the seemingly discrete segments of the world we inhabit and have felt that we should act from this stance in solving problems concerned with the well-being of our planet. It requires a leap in our thinking to realize that the methods we rationally use to "solve" planetary problems may unwittingly increase our alienation, so that we create a severely limited model of the nature of the relationship between ourselves and our world.

As we extend our dowsing ability, we need to question whether our goal is to increase the reach of our minds or merely to increase the complexity of our limitations. Even though we have only a limited awareness of reality, we must still act and make decisions, and this can become a terrifying responsibility until we build a basis of confidence within our limitations. We need to keep in mind that our search for a level of consciousness that encompasses our entire planet is nothing less than our search for Reality, for the authentic Reality that underlies the limited, apparent reality upon which we base our conventional lives.

Only when we have developed "right attitude" toward self, others, and the world—all linked together—have we reached the stage at which we can positively affect fields of subtle resonance that will then lead the self, others, and the world toward a state of creative harmony. Free from old habits of argument and confrontation, we can then begin to establish the habit of wholeness and to realize that the dowser, the target, and the dowsing process are not separate "things" but are merely different manifestations of a more fundamental reality.

In summary:

We are made of the stuff of the planet.

We and the planet are made from the same enfolded energies.

We, the planet, and the enfolded energies are all reflections of a single creative impulse.

We and all that exists are the products of that impulse, and, in a holographic sense, also *are* that impulse.

By working with the self and clarifying our attunement on all levels, we can attain a creative resonance with that single creative impulse.

Everything we do affects everything else, so we must be mindful of everything we do.

As we involve ourselves in planetary consciousness and use dowsing as a tool to help us seek the authentic self within, we find that we are then ready to enter the path of creative service to all the beings that are a part of our world.

9

STEWARDSHIP

In many traditions the subtle heart is referred to as an organ of consciousness. Joseph Chilton Pearce has called the physical heart "the physiological modus operandi for a wave form process which we call the subtle heart." When the ego and this subtle heart are merged, so are the human and the divine merged and that is "what human development is all about."[10]

Learning to integrate our individual ego selves into the subtle heart of universal consciousness is also what planetary consciousness and stewardship are all about. The more we understand the whole, the better we understand the relationship of the parts to the whole and realize that both our awareness and our actions need to spring from that sense of the whole, of which we are both part and (at least in a holographic sense) totality. Once aware of this amazing paradoxical heritage of the human being—that we experience individuality at the same time that we have the potential to be conscious of the greater unity—it becomes our responsibility to manifest this awareness to the degree of our understanding in all that we do.

Although the idea of interconnection has been part of the teachings of all authentic spiritual traditions, this concept still seems periodically to need to be rediscovered, and in this time of ecological crisis we have daily warnings about consequences of acting and thinking in nonconnected ways. Separation and alienation have marked our time. Most people generally still view family, friends, and perhaps family pets as within a circle, with the rest of the world outside—to be viewed with suspicion and often fear as alien others, competitors, or objects to be used. Most human institutions, including governments, continue to reflect this attitude. Even preservation organizations usually have very limited goals, so that when thoughts of shepherding resources for the future do occur, the animals, trees, plants, and rocks are themselves rarely considered; instead concern is mostly for their potential future "usefulness" to human beings.

In contrast, the world's indigenous peoples do not consider the complex interrelationship of beings and systems that we call nature in only this fragmented and utilitarian way. Interdependence of human beings with other life forms is recognized and expressed as brotherhood and sisterhood with all beings, and wonder and awe are felt for the diversity and power inherent in nature. Some more generally known religious traditions also have greater awareness of nature than do others; in some, nature is considered to be sacred, the "Book" of God, with all lessons contained therein for those who can learn to read them. But it has become a seldom-questioned assumption of our time and place to think of nature first as a commodity bank.

In *Science and the Modern World* Alfred North Whitehead wrote of the great influence that unquestioned assumptions have on an epoch. These assumptions include all those things we take for granted and about which we feel "that's the way it is." Some of these unquestioned assumptions (or at least those questioned by comparatively few) have helped to determine the ways in which in our time so many have come to relate in an I-it manner to the earth and to their fellow beings on the planet. Once aware of the need for change, we have been taught that we have the responsibility to do what we can to help, no matter how limited our contributions may be. Yet even more important than any actions that we take are the attitudes that surround those actions.

How we relate to our fellow creatures and to the world in which we live reveals much about our stage of vision and realization. Not only is much of our society's heartless treatment of animals in the food industry and for medical experimentation symptomatic of its immaturity of understanding, but so is the way many of us relate to the land itself. People put buildings where they do not belong, clear-cut forests, ignore or do not recognize the sacred places of the planet, and sacrifice the integrity of the whole for short-term goals.

As we awaken from the conditioning of our time and place and begin to question those still mostly unquestioned assumptions of our epoch, we will be able to begin to assume responsibility for what we as individuals can do something about.

In addition, as students of dowsing and also of a spiritual path, we have been made aware of the divine spark within everyone and everything and of our potential to move beyond what we previously might have accepted as our limitations, in a progressive expansion of consciousness that is really only limited by the limits we place upon it. "Human" means "God-conscious," and God-consciousness is our goal. Through reexamining our conditioning, we have the possibility of building our lives anew, and in dowsing we have a tool to help us to do this. Looking at those assumptions of our society about the treatment of animals and of land, if we don't feel or dowse that what is being done is right, then we can try to do something to change the situation. Many practical actions can be taken, but the most profound changes will come from helping to change consciousness, and, of course, this must begin with our own.

In our relationship to the animal world, each one of us must decide what seems for us right action. As a result of dowsed responses, some may want to reconsider their use of products tested on animals. Some may decide to be vegetarians. Some may decide that it is all right to eat meat if the animals whose lives are taken are treated with respect and their deaths accomplished without cruelty—and then work to see that whatever changes we dowse are appropriate are made. When we must take life, whether animal or vegetable, we can at least learn to do so with reverence and gratitude for the gift and by seeing that our lives manifest it in concern for the whole; and we can attempt through example to share our realization with others. These might be first steps toward recognizing that we are a part of, and also dependent upon, the whole—a thought well expressed in this grace by J. G. Bennett:

> All life is one
> and everything that lives is holy:
> Plants, animals and men.
> All must eat to live
> and to nourish one another.
> We bless the lives
> that have died to give us food.
> Let us eat consciously,
> resolving by our work to pay
> the debt of our own existence.[11]

James Lovelock's book *Gaia: A New Look at Life on Earth* suggests that the entire planet is a living organism of which all living things are a part. This concept has helped many people to begin to rethink that paradigm in which we are considered the lords of all we survey. While we do have a unique and royal role among living things, we feel that it is in the sense of responsibility rather than of exploitation—as custodians of our planet and of our fellow living beings, animal and plant and mineral. In a sense we are all Noah with the ark; to some degree the fate of all lives seems now to be in our charge.[12]

How we meet this challenge depends on the level of con-sciousness at which we are functioning—how we perceive the world and what we project by our thoughts and actions to contribute to it. For example, when we learn about hands-on healing, we learn that whatever energies are projected go through those of the "healer," just as, when we see other people's auras, we are looking at them as filtered through our own auras. Our efforts to act as stewards also have filters, and so once again we are brought back to the thought that to create what we think should be, we must begin with ourselves in a consistent aim to purify our egos and to integrate them into the subtle heart of universal consciousness.

Many people allow themselves to be locked into their own mental prisons, their assurance about "the way it's always been done." For example, we have all heard that "there has to be animal experimentation"; yet much so-called research on ani-mals has been shown to be frivolous—painful experiments that elicit only trivial information. For those experiments justified by some because their results ostensibly contribute to modern allopathic medicine, there are alternatives. One is dowsing the answers to important questions instead of doing experiments to answer them. And much anguish could be avoided for both people and animals by dowsing the results of painful and debilitating diagnostic tests instead of inflicting these on already stressed organisms. Of course, accuracy in such dowsing re-quires dedicated students willing to devote the time necessary to acquire skill and to build up track records. And also required are those medical professionals attuned to such projects and able to contribute the expertise to formulate the questions to be asked—a critical part of any project since, as we have learned, the answer is in the question.

Stages of dowsing competence appear to mirror our understanding of stages of awareness. If we dowse or live from only the level of personal consciousness, we remain at a primitive stage of what is possible for human beings. There are many stages, and we can perhaps recognize where we are on our life journeys by the kinds of dowsing skills that are natural for us and by the degree to which we are able to recognize the Oneness behind the multiplicity and the interconnectedness of all beings and all things. When we organize our thoughts and actions toward wholeness, the field of our intention will help to draw us toward our goal.

In *The Raiment of Light, A Study of the Human Aura,* David Tansley referred to the Sufi concept of the man of light. Writing about this concept in *The Man of Light in Iranian Sufism,* Henry Corbin said, "*New senses* perceive *directly* the order of reality corresponding to them. At this stage, in fact, the intellect realizes how deceptive are the senses which previously suggested to it that nothing is real except what is physically seen, tasted and touched."[13] The spiritual body of resurrection is understood in this Sufi tradition to be the body of light that we gradually may unveil; the subtle heart is its center. In dowsing we can also use as a goal the unveiling of the man or woman of light within and the transmuting of our senses into organs of light, into suprasensory senses.

There is a dervish saying that to look at the sun you must have eyes like the sun. Dowsing can help us to search for different ways to solve problems by changing the eyes with which we see—and the ways we relate to everything.

Being a better dowser means learning to live in greater harmony with the earth and all her beings. It means asking what is the Divine intention and then helping to manifest it. In so doing, we may become what Reshad Feild calls "transformers of subtle energy"—with the capacity truly to be able to serve.

When we look at a problem, we also need to look for the

qualities—what we're intended to learn—being called forth by that particular situation, both in us and in the people we are attempting to aid. How can we help in the evolution of the people involved through the dowsing search? Just doing clearings of discarnates or noxious zones without helping the individuals involved to see what was behind those symptoms— what the situation was intended to teach—is perhaps to interfere with the programming of the universe. As Pir Vilayat Inayat Khan says, "The purpose behind the programming of the universe . . . is not that things will run smoothly. . . . The purpose is that people should progress and gain realization. In order to make that possible, people have to be tested."[14] If being tested is necessary for realization, then we want to make sure that we don't just treat symptoms that may be there to move the person toward understanding an underlying cause, or even a purpose behind the cause. We want to help people to take their appropriate next steps in personal evolution. By teaching people how to ask questions and to explore context, we may be able to help them to see some of their problems as teacup tempests and to release them from these to a larger consciousness, a process which will in itself be healing.

Much has been written about the "hundredth monkey" phenomenon: after a certain number have learned something new, others (even distant in space) seem to know it too. Through this story and through knowing about morphogenetic fields, we can understand that an effect can be brought about by concerted thought by even a comparatively few people. Much has also been written about what is called the "Maharishi effect," in which a few TM meditators in a city have seemed to bring down the crime rate or to ease international tensions.

A thought is a thing; we can dowse the field created by a thought. When a group of people come together with their thoughts, as they do, for example, in prayer, we can dowse that the field created is much greater than the sum of its parts. Dowsers joined together with positive thoughts can have a helpful effect on our world, and increasingly so as the dowsers themselves become more realized and the beneficial power they have is thereby increased.

Peace is everyone's concern for the planet, but peace, after all, is not a goal but a process—the result of how things are thought about and done. To approach a state of planetary consciousness—harmony with the universe—means reconciling ourselves with the land and with our fellow creatures, drawing the circle to include all with compassion and love, using our divine heritage as was intended—as earth stewards and peacekeepers.

10

WATER

We can't help being thirsty,
moving toward the voice
of water.[15]

—*Rumi*

When someone speaks of dowsing, a listener usually thinks first of water. And learning to dowse is best done, we feel, by beginning to dowse basic verifiable targets. This usually means starting with water and sewer lines and then moving on to dowse for water domes and water veins, as described in detail in *The Divining Mind.* Water dowsing is vital to learn because it is a way to locate potable water, for which there is increasing need. Water is crucial to life; people and most animals can live a long time without food but only a relatively short time without water. Not only is there concern worldwide for dwindling water tables (rising population and spreading industrialization take increasing tolls on supplies), but the quality of groundwater almost everywhere is declining rapidly. Few cities now have good water and even country springs and wells are often polluted. Chemicals and pesticides carried on the winds rain down and filter into ground supplies. Surface spraying also means that pesticides leach into wells. Untreated sewage too often flows into streams, lakes, and oceans.

Dowsers trained by the American Society of Dowsers look not for surface or groundwater but instead for veins of primary water flowing from water domes. This *primary water* is understood to rise from deep in the earth until stopped by an obstacle such as ledge; blocked from further rising at that point, the water flows out at different depths in veins. This water is perceived as pure unless it has traveled through a contaminant. In their searches, dowsers program—among other stipulations—for the purest possible drinking water and for year-round flow. The importance of being able to find this kind of water is obvious.

Water is so much a part of our being and so much a part of the world we perceive that we often take it for granted; but, as with anything else that at first seems comparatively simple, when we begin to try to understand more of its nature, we find great complexity.

Beyond the utilitarian link between dowsers and water there is a more subtle relationship between the human being and water.[16] Our bodies are made up largely of water. We start life in a watery sac, and many of our folkloric, mythic, and spiritual understandings and symbols have to do with water.

Creation is from water and Spirit. Death has sometimes been described as a setting forth across water to the world beyond and new life. Water has traditionally been a symbol of life and is used in consecrations and testings, separating good from evil, truth from falsehood. It is the first-choice medium for ablutions, ritual cleansing to prepare one for communion with God. With the world tree beside it, the sacred spring or fountain—the water of life from which all rivers flow—is at the center of paradise. Without water there is desert, so fertility and abundance signify the presence of water. If it is lacking, the quest—a spiritual quest—is to find it. A universal theme in folktale and literature is the "freeing of the waters," the ending of drought and the restoration of the waters and so the land to fruitfulness.

The motif of the cup has many associations with water. In the Tarot the suit of cups stood for the water element, to be replaced later in the deck of playing cards by the symbol of the heart. In Celtic tradition the magic cup from the sea would break if three lies were spoken over it, so there is the association of truth with it; the Celtic cauldron possessed the power of regeneration. Both water and cup are used as symbols of the feminine. Mary is sometimes called Star of the Sea or the Sealed Fountain.

The dowser with his wand recalls Moses striking the rock from which water flowed. The forked stick, traditionally cut from a tree with an affinity to water, incorporates the idea of the sacred tree as well.

In the Christian tradition baptism in or by water creates the new man, reborn to enter the kingdom of God. As we thirst for water, so do we thirst for God, whose water washes away sins and whose flood destroys in order to cleanse and allow regeneration. Khidr, the archetypal Green Man and Guide of the Sufis, is associated with Elijah and with the Water of Life.

In the Jungian reading of the alchemical tradition, the philosopher's stone is understood as the "water" from which all comes and in which all is contained. *Solutio* is to turn a solid into a liquid, back to the *prima materia*.[17] *Solve et coagula*—to dissolve the current limited sense of oneself and re-form it with an expanded sense of self—is the purpose of meditation done in what is called an alchemical retreat process: dissolving allows the death of unwanted aspects of the ego, and is followed by regeneration.

One way to learn to dowse for water is in some sense to "become" water. If one explores this thought, then one can learn from the element water much about how to live.

Water can help us to understand how we are related to the earth, for we can think of water as the circulatory system of the planet, also manifesting in its parts. In *Sensitive Chaos*, Theodor Schwenk describes how the plant world plays its role in the circulation of water; on a summer's day, he says, 3500 gallons are "drawn through an acre of woodland into the atmosphere. . . . Together earth, plant world and atmosphere form a *single* great organism, in which water streams like living blood." Animals and people have this same kind of system within themselves "in a small space, where it moves in just such rhythms and according to just such laws as the water outside in nature."[18] Schwenk also points out that water, with no "inherent form of its own," is yet the "matrix of all metamorphoses of form."[19] (A *matrix* is that within which and from which something takes form.)

For Viktor Schauberger, a forester who studied water all his life, "living water" meant a specific kind of water. At its highest quality, it has a temperature of four degrees Celsius and on clear cold nights can carry its greatest load of logs. He found that water responds to forest and shade and advised that watercourses should not be straightened. A natural watercourse builds up an energy that flows within the stream in the opposite way and can be seen as a channel of light within the stream. Trout or salmon travel upstream within this energy flow.[20]

Schauberger said that water, a living, naturally spiralling substance, can also die; unfortunately, we are now seeing the dying of many rivers of the world. If living water is the only healthy kind of water to drink, very few have access to such water. Schauberger devised a way to put the spiral form back into water and to transport it in piping that continued this form. His understanding of water has not yet had the attention it deserves.

In addition to being a major part of ourselves and of our

world, water has a fundamental role in keeping us in a state of health and balance and has been used in healing since ancient times. The spiritual importance of water is at the very heart of life as well as of the dowsing art.

Reshad Feild says in *Here to Heal* that "Water . . . is a conductor of electricity, and thought-forms are electrical impulses."[21] Moisture is carried on the breath. Feild has also said that healing can be effected by changing the molecular structure of water,[22] and we think that all changes that the dowser makes through thought alone may be effected through the medium of water, with the "sound of" thought—the vibration of thought—on the "water" of the breath "fixing" pattern much as the pattern of vibration is "fixed" on a Chladni plate. (Ernst Chladni sprinkled sand on steel disks and observed the changing patterns as various notes were played on a violin.)[23]

Water is also used as a physical carrier of energies used in healing and centering: as the vehicle for flower essences; in biodynamic preparations; in "treated" water given to people, animals, and plants by spiritual healers; and in holy water and in holy wells, where the surrounding thought-forms enhance the natural and special qualities of the water.

As we begin to learn, we realize that water is the mother of all, symbol of our source and our regeneration—a simple thing, a necessary part of all life, and yet with enormous complexity. Water dowsers wear the mantle of all these associations as they go out in quest of what always is the water of life.

11

EARTH ENERGIES

One aspect of our stewardship role is to learn about earth energies. However, talks and writings on earth energies recall the blind men in the familiar story, each one describing the whole elephant as inferred from only the part he is touching. Our paradigms must continually be revised as new information comes to us or as we perceive new ways of understanding information we already have. So this is the first point to be made about earth energies: we have intriguing clues but we do not yet have the whole picture; the way in which we put information together may have to change when we understand more.

In our paradigm the earth is indeed a living being, a place of wonders far beyond childhood fantasies, a nurturing place to be, and a continuing school. And we are seemingly provided with all that we need as we learn how to live here in harmony. The physical apparency of the world, this solid-seeming secondary reality with its usual concerns, is not all that is really happening here—in this paradigm. Growing awareness of what is behind what appears naturally brings about an increasing desire to live in greater harmony with and service to the Divine Plan.

For many of us the first appeal in hearing about earth energies was the hint that in learning about them we would be learning about the master plan of a "golden age" of love, harmony, and beauty, and so would be able to re-create it and repair some of the damage done to the earth. As we become more involved in the study of earth energies, and open ourselves through dowsing to what unfolds as an increasingly complex network of forces, we also become less certain of being able to comprehend the whole pattern, and more filled with wonder that there could have been so many clues hidden in plain sight, ignored by so many for so long. Perhaps the complexity is intended to frustrate our rational sense and push us forward into a new mode of consciousness in the way that a Zen koan can. However, we are still in the stage of naming the parts. More and more kinds of earth energies are being noted or named or, worse, lumped together under the same name, making it all very confusing.

It is still not always clear whether we are dowsing and talking about forces that are measurable within the generally accepted scientific paradigm, forces that are "real" but not measurable in this way, or, in some cases, subjective reactions to thought-forms or thought-forms mirrored. Before they first search for a water vein, for example, we train beginning dowsers to clear for previous random thought-forms that consciously or unconsciously may have been imposed upon the landscape. But we also have learned that a thought is a thing. We know that thought alone, when it is in resonance, can result in what many people would call miracles. Distinctions between thought and material target become blurred, with differences that must be understood to be arbitrary or of degree.

Various groups and individuals are investigating earth energies with instrumentation. But since most of these efforts are designed within the paradigm of conventional science, it seems likely that these attempts can be only in small part useful because of limitations in understanding reflected in both apparatus and design of experiment.

Therefore, we come back to "judgment by results." We can, for example, dowse changes in the auras of human beings standing on various earth currents. Auras are nearly invisible fields of subtle energy that surround the body; every living and some hand-made things have dowseable auras. The basic procedure of dowsing an aura is, with a dowsing tool, to walk toward the subject, who first stands in a place of neutral earth energies. Ask that the edge of a particular aura (for example, what is sometimes called the health aura) be indicated as the tool reaches it (L-rods would swing open, a pendulum would circle). This procedure then can be repeated over a dowsed noxious water vein or on an energy ley, and definite differences in the dowsed auras will be seen: the aura will be constricted over the harmful energy and expanded over the energy ley, although many factors (such as state of health and degree of fatigue) may cause variations as well. After a while the new dowser will begin to feel the differences in these energies automatically, through recognizing his or her own subtle body signals. There are places that feel good to be in, that expand our awareness, that help us to realize our link to the sacred; and there are spots where we just don't feel good, places that make us ill, places where vegetation doesn't thrive and the smell is unpleasant. These places are usually those where human beings have not understood the earth energies, have built in the wrong places, have blasted with dynamite (thereby blocking subtle flows), or have harmed fellow creatures in some way. When harmed land is "healed," it again smells good and feels good to be on.

To learn to live in harmony with the earth requires that, with attention and love, we ask to be made aware of the Divine intention in all that we do. We ask what the land wants to express at a particular time rather than just imposing our wills upon it. We ask the permission questions. We learn to refine our dowsing questions.

Earth energies are invisible to most people, and so we are dependent on asking cogent questions and on clearly differentiating mentally among things in our dowsing searches. We get what we ask for, so it is important to understand terms that often vary in meaning according to the user. Here, therefore, is a partial catalog of our own tentative personal understanding of some of the terms related to earth energies.

First is the term *energy* itself. We may think of energy as that out of which everything has been formed. Energy implies power, and power is associated with work performed. In earth-energy study, the work is vague; what is referred to by "energy" is something that has a dowseable "power" (permits a dowseable response) and that may be indicated by other landscape signs once one learns to read them. This "power" may once have been more fully understood and utilized, and dowsers are interested in learning about it.

The earth energies that you are likely to hear and read about most frequently, along with phenomena connected with them, are *energy ley lines.* Other names sometimes used for what may possibly be the same force, or different aspects of it, are power lines, earth rays, overgrounds, earth currents, and geodetic lines. Perhaps you remember an Irish folktale in which a corner of a house had to be cut off so as not to obstruct a fairy path; "fairy path" also may be another way to say "energy ley."

The term *ley* came into popular use with Alfred Watkins, who was not the first to note alignments of sites but did, in the 1920s, popularize awareness that significant old sites in England could be connected with straight lines. More interest was stirred up in 1969 when John Michell's *The View Over Atlantis* was published. Over the years many people have sought alignments of sites, charting them on survey maps. A rule of thumb has become that if there are five significant sites on a ten-mile line, the alignment may be called a ley. Significant points can be such things as megalithic sites, springs, sacred groves, wells, stone circles, moats, mounds, crosses, and medieval churches. Features presently on the sites may be from different historical periods, because later monuments were often built on sites that earlier were marked as significant.

Terry Ross discovered that in the United States there were similar straight lines, that these were dowseable, and that visualizing or walking along them one could discover standing stones and stone chambers. Many of the Vermont stone chambers, for example—those that were not built for use as root cellars or burial vaults (although they may later have been used in that way)—are on energy leys.

Energy leys or *E-leys* are terms coined by Sig Lonegren to differentiate alignments with dowseable earth energy from those that at present do not seem to have dowseable energy. Most American writers who mention leys mean what Sig Lonegren calls energy leys.

The basic American understanding of energy leys has been that they are usually lines of force six to eight feet wide that come in from space, make a ninety-degree turn and travel in a straight line, then exit at ninety degrees into the earth (or we think sometimes back into the sky). The width of the lines seems to vary—or at least such is dowsing perception of them—according to time of day, moon, and year, and there is a dowseable direction of flow (or what some perceive as currents flowing in opposite ways, as there are in natural watercourses). Primary water coming from a blind spring (another name for a dome)—pure water coming from deep in the earth—is dowsed where the energy leys come to earth and exit and where they cross. Where an energy ley and underground water meet, there is potential for what is termed a *power point,* a place where a person may experience an expansion of consciousness. Where a number of energy leys cross over water, a very powerful situation is created. Many old and sacred structures of the world are found where energy leys and water meet. It is not agreed as to whether the stone marking of the sites brought the water to them or whether it was there all along.

Terry Ross has referred to a ley as "a dowseable line of force several feet wide and extending various distances, over which man has built some of his noblest works. Perhaps it's a helical spin travelling close to the speed of light. Sometimes [the leys] seem to be in a hexagonal grid pattern six miles on a side."[24]

The pattern of the leys has interested many. Joseph Heinsch thought that the lines running through the Rhineland formed vast runes that imbued the district with their magical attributes. He also felt that holy hills were the starting points for ley lines, and many writers in the earth-energies field associate the earth's force systems with holy mountains and also relate ley lines to a crystal grid pattern on the earth.

Confusion occurs because the whole network of subtle forces to which dowsers have opened is still subjective, and each person brings to it individual awareness of a different part of the "elephant" recognized and an individual conception of what each term means. Some dowsers call everything but water ley energy. Some call the highest known intensities of these lines energy leys but do not use that name for force that behaves similarly but is not as strong as are the energy leys in the great spiritual centers where human intent has been focused over many years. Some English dowsers speak of leys, meaning energy leys, by color, and there is confusion when a black stream is mentioned as to whether a water vein or an energy ley is meant.

The energy-ley pattern appears not to be static, and, in addition to their changing width, energy leys come and go. Our collie friend Brigit frequently directed our notice to changes in the energy pattern in our yard. One way she did this was to walk around, instead of across, an area where a new energy coming down or going up had appeared. We noted this and, when we dowsed, found that there had been this change in the energy pattern.

What does it mean when the whole energy-ley complex shifts

a few feet this way or that or when the whole pattern changes? Sometimes we do not yet know the right questions to ask.

Some dowsers feel, when they are making requests for healing, that they have some connection with the energy-ley system. Being in or thinking of being in a powerful place when one is making a healing prayer does seem to add strength to the request.

Some dowsers imply that ley lines may be harmful to health; as we understand energy-ley power, it is power—neither positive nor negative in essence—but with the ability to put a person further along in the direction already taken. An energy ley can be a wonderful place for short-term meditation, but it may also be harmful to one who is unbalanced, because an energy ley tends to amplify a person's current state. One wouldn't deliberately build a house on an energy-ley complex, although, for example, if the home becomes a spiritual teaching center it is possible that lines will come into it on their own. Energy leys appear to amplify intent, with all the implications of that statement, and anyone spending time on them needs to be centered and clear.

Another kind of energy that we recognize is what we call *ch'i lines*. These are curved lines that seem to be similar to acupuncture meridians in the human body—not so surprising if the earth is a living being. The good energies of ch'i lines appear to attract to them, or to be vehicles for, visions from other planes. But when this energy is blocked (as through blasting), the blocked energy becomes harmful to health.

There is a whole very complicated study of curving earth energies called *feng shui,* literally "wind" and "water." It was once very popular in China and is now finding interest widely, with many books currently available in English on aspects of this science. After working through a very complicated procedure, a feng shui practitioner plans the harmonious placement of a tomb or a home or a business, or of furnishings within a building.

Feng shui is one system of *geomancy*, which—as the term is

used in connection with earth energies—is a study that includes how to build in the right place at the right time in order to live in harmony with both the earth and the heavens.

The idea in feng shui is that ch'i is exhaled by the mountains and circles through the macrocosm. Where ch'i can freely circulate there are fragrance and beauty and people live harmoniously; where it is stopped from circulating, natural products above it will be "bitter" and people evil and foolish. The essence of good feng shui is to accumulate ch'i without letting it become torpid. The ideal geomantic house placement is a site nestled in the hills with trees to the north and with a view to the south. Ideally, water should flow gently in front of the site and the landforms should unite what feng shui practitioners call white tiger (feminine) energies of the west and azure dragon (masculine) energies of the east.

In *Sun and Serpent* Hamish Miller and Paul Broadhurst wrote of tracking two curving lines of force, which they have named the Michael and Mary currents, across Great Britain. Although they didn't call them by our name, it would appear to us that these undulating lines are what we would call ch'i lines rather than energy leys, which we think of as being always straight. Until we had read their book we had not thought to differentiate between a masculine and a feminine kind of ch'i, although there is this kind of differentiation in feng shui. Once we had thought to dowse whether a particular ch'i line had qualities that could be described by gender, we received an affirmative answer. This is a good example of one of the ways we learn to ask the dowsing questions that will expand our knowledge—by noting what others are finding and then dowsing how that applies to our own understanding.

We use the term *noxious ch'i* for ch'i lines that have been blocked by inappropriate human action. For example, we learned from Reshad Feild that it appears that blasting can cause damage at a location many miles from the blasting site. One discovers this in dowsing when, in asking for the source of a local problem, one finds that it is many miles away. Every act of violence on the earth leaves its mark until it is healed. What happens on a noxious ch'i line? Accidents happen; things go wrong. As acupuncture can be used to free sluggish energy in the body, so is it possible to use acupuncture of the earth to enable the earth currents again to flow. If on the physical plane, this must be done very precisely or it can cause even more harm; it is not work for beginners. What happens when this acupuncture is done after receiving all the permissions and by someone trained to do it? The wind and temperature change, a sweet smell comes, and the feeling on the land, the "luck," changes. This kind of healing of the land can be done by some with prayer.

Ch'i appears to flow on its own and with or near water. Noxious radiations from some water and mineral veins, we believe, sometimes cause and almost always exacerbate disease. Yet, all water veins do not seem to us to have noxious radiations connected with them. There are different theories about the harmful energy; some think it is from water veins up to a certain depth; others, that it is blocked, negative ch'i energy nearby that affects the water. In any case, the energy of "noxious" water veins is a decomposing energy. It is very suitable to site a compost heap over such a water vein, but it is not such a good place for your bed or favorite chair.

In Europe doctors are much more aware of the havoc caused by noxious water veins under homes; in this country these geopathic zones as a factor in health are virtually unknown by most of the medical profession. After simply moving a bed or a frequently used chair, very often there will be an amazingly co-incidental recession of a person's symptoms of arthritis, for example. There are also ways dowsers can help to block or remove the harmful effects of such veins. These ways include staking the veins, which means pounding rebar (metal rods) into the earth in dowsed locations—the stakes perhaps really being symbols of thought-forms, "anchored" by sound. Or a vein may be moved through hammering against the side of a metal stake dowsed both for its positioning and for the number of hammer strokes. Some dowsers may eventually find that they can bring about the same results through prayer, when it is appropriate to do so and all the permissions have been received.

We would like to underline the thought that the harmful effects of some water veins, noxious ch'i lines, and some mineral veins can be attributed to lack of knowledge and abuse of nature. We build where we have no business to build. We damage the earth with practices such as blasting in ways that affect earth currents, about which most of us have no knowledge but that affect us whether we know about them or not. We have a great deal to learn from people who have lived more lightly on the land.

In feng shui, as we understand it, straight lines are anathema, an idea that appears to contradict what we seem to be finding out about the energy ley system. Joseph R. Jochmans some years ago suggested that we now have only part of the feng shui system and that straight lines perhaps had to do with imperial power. This is an idea also expressed in Sun and Serpent.

The seat of government was once thought to be of necessity in the country's sacred spot. "When the king's throne is in the right place, there is no quarreling with the king."[25] But a sacred spot may be created by the consciousness we bring to it, and it does appear that the energy ley system follows consciousness.

Geomancy is the awakening of consciousness to the process of bringing human activities into harmony and resonance with the earth and with the cosmos. Rupert Sheldrake put it another way when he said, "Geomancy is the science of understanding interactive flows within fields."[26] The net of interrelationships is always much more intricate than we can understand with our rational minds, and so, before we dowse, we ask permission of the Source so that anything we do will be harmonious and within the balance of nature.

We want to learn to become sensitive to what the land wants to express and to assist in this expression. In feng shui the Chinese had a very complex understanding of the harmony of earth and heaven. Other peoples have also had their own understanding of geomancy, and some still do. Native American traditions recognize and respect as sacred certain places and especially certain mountains. Australian Aborigines use songlines (stories of places as they travel) to connect them with landscape features and with the Dreamtime. As a place is considered sacred generation after generation, there is a process of morphic resonance connecting across time and space, for "fields have memory," as Rupert Sheldrake has said.[27] Memory is and means resonance, and a sacred place, whether marked by a building or not, has much to teach if we are able to connect resonantly with it.

Native Americans knew how to site their worship and living spaces in right relationship with the earth currents. We have been told that the dowsing of old pictures of encampments has shown that no water veins flowed under the tipis and that energy leys could be found only through the tipi of the medicine man or shaman, who knew how to use their power. Recently in this country, however, most of the building has been done by people knowing nothing, either by training or by intuition, about geomancy. Buildings and roads are put in any location, with no awareness whatsoever of disrupted earth currents or what the effects of this disruption may be. When disease and trouble follow, dowsers interested in earth energies are sometimes asked to try to make repairs. But how much better it would be if architects and contractors would build with awareness in the first place. We do what we can when we are asked and have permission and, in so doing, we also do what we can to make people more aware of the importance of learning about geomancy.

12

INTENT

As we learn to dowse, mistakes we make and the kinds of problems we are given require the learning of ever more detail and precision in framing questions. Inevitably, however, there comes a time when we become uncertain about our capacity to know. Sensing the inadequacy of our present understanding, we must then ask that our intention override our limitations. An example of this situation exists regarding what many dowsers call noxious water veins.

We know that so-called noxious water veins seem to exacerbate the physical (and mental, though we don't hear so much about that) condition of people who spend lots of time over them, as in bed or in a favorite chair. Although the greatest interest in this phenomenon so far has been in Europe, some American dowsers have also made studies correlating severe illness and proximity to underground water veins. At the very least it appears that this kind of irritation zone is a stress on people that could be eliminated by a variety of means.

There are various theories proposed about what causes some water veins to be harmful to people. While the relationship of discarnate entities to water veins is not always mentioned, we feel it is very important. These trapped souls need to be released and sent on to their next proper place of development before any changes are made in these veins, and the presence of discarnates surely is a factor in the degree of toxicity experienced from these veins. Noxious (that is, damaged) ch'i energy in proximity to water veins seems to us to affect the water harmfully, but many dowsers do not dowse for this ch'i energy.

There has been objection by some to calling water veins noxious, libeling an aspect of nature in this way, because what is harmful to one form of life is not necessarily so to another. It is our present understanding that noxious energies associated with water in large part are caused because people do not have a true understanding of the world in which they live. If, in building houses and roads in ways that harm the earth's energies, blockages are created that impinge on nearby water veins, then it is perhaps not the water at all that is the problem. Water may, however, amplify the effect and we may choose to say it *is* the problem and use *noxious water vein* as a symbol of some network of relationships we don't yet really understand.

We have already mentioned that thought can be directed to change the molecular structure of water to bring about change or healing. If thought indeed has this affinity to water, may it not also be a contributing factor in the noxiousness associated with some water veins? Does water collect and hold thought, whether positive or negative? This possibility might help to explain, at least to those content with esoteric explanations, the seeming ease with which noxious water veins are so often brought back to harmony by thought alone. After recognizing noxiousness, asking the permissions, and requesting restoration of harmony, we very frequently have seen changes occur for the better in the health of beings living in proximity to such veins.

A key factor here seems to be recognition of at least part of what is out of harmony before things may be put right. A dowser beginning to work in such subtle realms gets endless lessons in the complexity of the web of life and the relationships within it in order to identify what is out of balance. This appears to be a necesssary part of the training—to become aware of great complexity before we are able to reach a stage of higher simplicity. At first literalness and precision of the question seem necessary. Later, however, intention sometimes overrides this literalness. This appears to happen only when a certain opening of the heart has occurred—when the dowser has moved along in understanding of the earth steward role, with its attendant responsibility toward the well-being of all creatures, and when he or she is engaged in true service. A vague "good intention" when making requests is not the same thing; the purity of such vague intention may be more clouded than an individual knows.

In dowsing a noxious water vein, we remember that the water itself may not be the culprit, but may merely be mirroring in some way the disharmony of something else. But being of right intent, having asked the permissions and received them, and then acting *as if* it were emanations from the water vein that need to be detoxified, the experienced dowser may make a request and have the wished-for result occur whether or not there has been total precision in the request. At least we must feel that a result has occurred when, after the request, there is an improvement in the health of the people living in proximity to the vein.

A further manifestation of this resonant phenomenon is when advanced dowsers use just a personal symbol to represent what previously they had gone through in detail or, in even more advanced dowsing, when they just bring a situation to mind and it is taken care of without anything specific even being asked. There appears to be some kind of synchronicity involved, some kind of contact with a field established in primary reality, that allows this to happen and that seems to be directly attendant upon the consciousness of the dowser and the dowser's resonance with the target. When he or she is in resonance with the wholeness of creation, the dowser appears to have cooperation from the invisible worlds in what needs to be done, and as the dowser comes closer and closer to resonating with the Creative Will, the simpler everything becomes.

When his or her consciousness allows transparency to what Terry Ross calls "everywhere and everywhen," and to the degree that it allows that transparency and has resonance with all creation, then will the dowser be able to manifest what Joseph Chilton Pearce has called the "power of consciousness related to possibility."[28] This, as we see it, is the creative potential of dowsing.

PART FOUR

ATTENTION AND HEALING: INVOLVING STAGES FOUR THROUGH SIX AND BEYOND

✳

The world is full of remedies,
but you have no remedies until God
opens a window for you.
Though you are unaware of that remedy now,
God will make it clear
in the hour of need.[29]

—*Rumi*

But ask now the beasts,
and they shall teach thee;
and the fowls of the air,
and they shall tell thee:
Or speak to the earth,
and it shall teach thee:
and the fishes of the sea
shall declare unto thee.

—*Job 12: 7–8*

13

PRAYER AND HEALING THE HUMAN BEING

Many people are attracted to the potential that dowsing has for aid in areas of health and healing. There are, however, dangers in trying to be a healing presence before one is truly ready. In fact, much damage is done by those who assume a knowledge they don't have and who try, without permission, to impose their will as to what should be onto people, animals, plants, or the land itself. Their effect may be very different from what they think they are doing. It is because of such irresponsible behavior that stringent laws exist in many states regarding unqualified (as defined within the current medical system) attempts to "heal." Although these laws can inappropriately block much help that could otherwise be given, and although in many cases it would be beneficial if they were revised, one has only to see the harm caused by some individuals to understand why these laws were drawn up in the first place.

The principal reason for educating people about the interface of dowsing and consciousness is to facilitate the efforts of those who truly want to be of service. What they will be learning to do is, as we understand it, appropriate within present law; it will enable them to work regardless of proximity to their subjects; and any "healing" that is elicited through their efforts will be from the highest level, for what we are talking about is prayer.

In *Recovering the Soul* Dr. Larry Dossey wrote of an experiment on patients in the cardiology unit of San Francisco General Hospital. Nearly half the selected group were prayed for; slightly more were not. The experiment results showed that of the two groups, those prayed for needed significantly less medical intervention. Also, it appeared from the study that distance between the patients and those praying for them was not significant, and neither was the form of the prayer used. Dr. Dossey also wrote of the Spindrift (Salem, Oregon) experiments on seeds and prayer, in which prayed-for seeds sprouted in greater numbers than those that were not prayed for. The Spindrift researchers found that the more the practitioner was aware of the subject being prayed for, the greater the effect, and that so long as the practitioner could hold in mind an "overall concept of the system involved," the effect of the prayer was constant over all its components. They also found that the most effective kind of prayer was "Thy will be done." Dr. Dossey noted that

> the *non*directed technique appeared quantitatively much more effective, frequently yielding results that were twice as great, or more, when compared to the directed approach. This may surprise persons who favor the techniques of directed imagery and visualization that are quite popular today.[30]

The Spindrift researchers, after tests "on a variety of biological systems," suggested that "the healer strive to be completely free of visualizations, associations, or specific goals."[31] (It is likely that the degree of attunement of those praying is the real differential and that, when visualizations are correctly directed, they are also effective. Others have found, however, that visualizations that are precise but not accurately directed can cause difficulties.[32])

Recovering the Soul is a timely reinforcement of what we have learned about the value of prayer in distant healing. Dr. Dossey recognizes the difficulty people have in assessing the role of prayer in health because of the view that

> prayer is manifestly futile on the grounds of distance alone, of spatial separation, aside from the fact that it is nonmaterial and "mental." . . .
>
> The bugbear of locality is everywhere and infiltrates everything we do in medicine today. Because we insist that all therapies be physically based, we are off to the technological races, as we have been for over a century. And with arguable results—for, echoed in the experience of everyone, patients *and* physicians, there is an increasing awareness that something has been left out.
>
> What has been omitted is the realization of who we are. Our therapies in medicine force us to assume the role of a purely local creature. But this is a false identity. It is a participation in hypocrisy, for it denies that we are nonlocal beings in space and time.[33]

The form of prayer that we use is based mostly on what we have learned from Terry Ross. His article in *The American Dowser* presented this method and is reprinted in full in the appendix.

In a typical healing prayer, the dowser attunes first to nonlocal mind, to the Highest and Best that he or she knows. A request has been made. If permission to the May I? Can I? Should I? questions is received, the dowser next asks whether there is entity incursion on the individual being prayed for. If there is, the dowser requests that any discarnate beings harmful to the health of the person involved be taken on to their next proper place of development.

The understanding here is that some beings who die do not go on as intended in the Divine Plan, but cling to the earth plane as discarnate entities, using human beings and noxious water veins as energy sources. Note that the dowser's intervention is not exorcism as it is usually understood; the beings are not "driven out," but a request is made that they be escorted to their next proper place of development—better for them as well as for the living person. Occasionally a discarnate being is here for a good purpose, so the dowser is careful to be specific about ones harmful (in terms of the highest good) to the health of the person for whom the prayer is made.

Next in the prayer, influence from noxious water veins is checked out, since these emanations have been found to exacerbate or precipitate disease. Any disturbances from mineral veins are also dowsed for, and it is requested that any harmful energies be detoxified. Please note that this step must always follow requests for the removal of harmful entities. Electrical loops, which appear to be loop-shaped fields of harmful energy related to electrical fields, are checked for and prayed about in the same way. Although somewhat imprecise, the symbolic use of the term *electrical loop* appears to produce the desired effect when requesting a positive clearing. We would also suggest checking for blocked ch'i lines and including at this point in the prayer a request for their return to harmony.

Then other spots that the person often visits and that may have harmful incursions are brought to mind, and protection from the harmful effects is requested.

The prayer then goes back in time, with dowsing for other places and times in the person's life, all the way back through the prenatal period. Harmful influences—specifically, harmful discarnate entities and noxious water veins—that were once experienced may still retain influence on the person in the present, and the prayer asks that the memories of these incursions be removed from the person's being.

The high self of the person being prayed for is contacted and asked whether or not that person forgives everyone who has caused him or her harm, asks forgiveness of any he or she may have harmed, and then forgives himself or herself. This threefold forgiveness appears necessary for the prayer to function fully. Then the prayer is made that the person be restored to a state of harmony, with all subtle bodies perfectly entrained and functioning appropriately. It is requested that all those who come in contact with the person, in the healing professions or at home, have his or her true best interests at heart and have appropriate skill in meeting his or her needs. Note that it is not specified what the physical outcome should be.

Thanks are given that the prayer has been heard and the person is released to the Will of God (or the Great Spirit). Some dowsers pray using "guides" or "angels" as intermediaries, and make their prayer from a "safe place"—a special "room" near a favorite beautiful spot, visualized for this purpose, where intermediaries are met and requests made. Part of the intent in this is to remove personal ego from the situation and to turn the requests over to those on higher planes who are able to handle them. This approach provides safety from involvement with planes and beings not fully understood and again clearly defines the requests as prayer.

Even though nothing is done beyond such a loving and simple prayer, amazing things are known to follow. The efficacy of the prayer, we are convinced, does not depend on the precise form or wording of the individual requests but on the degree to which the one praying truly is able to lovingly attune his or her thoughts to the patient and to the Wholeness that includes all. At that time the one praying is released from the boundaries of space and time that define the individual. When someone has done this kind of praying for years, a very powerful morphic field of habit is surely built up by the repeated focusing of intent. Eventually the dowser probably only has to bring the matter to mind, perhaps with some symbol to represent the process originally spelled out in detail, and the same result is obtained. To be able to pray effectively in this way requires absolutely clear loving intent—and the doing of it time after time.

While impediments for the most part unrecognized by allopathic medicine in this country have been identified in the dowsing search, requests for the restoration of harmony are pure prayer.

Of course, no financial compensation is accepted for personal use by the dowser for the prayer, although he or she does appreciate being told what happened after the prayer was made. This is not a matter of vanity but of learning, for there is always more to learn.

It needs to be remembered that "healing" may have manifestations other than physical healing. Always it is important to remember "Thy will be done," most especially when results are not what we in our rational mode would choose. At such times we may learn more about "that which transpires behind that which appears." Esoteric literature is full of reminders that no prayer is ever lost, although it may manifest in ways that we are then unable to comprehend. Intuition may suggest to us further questions to dowse so that we may better understand.

It is true that exceptional beings may heal by prayer or even by presence alone, without awareness of dowsing. These beings are in a high state of spiritual unfoldment and have the attunement or resonance that is part of that state. But this book is about the path of dowsing and how we may gradually unfold the capacity to access information enfolded in primary reality and later to effect change through moving from consciousness of our little selves to that of the greater Self of which we are all part. Larry Dossey calls this process "developing awareness of nonlocal mind" and explains:

when they share a paradigm of reality in which many planes of being are included. Many esoteric books have included information on discarnate beings, but now, as more books are being published in which mainstream authors write of these facts, awareness of these realities may soon be more common.

As we learned to dowse, we learned that most dowsers accept that there are other planes of existence with which we can interact and that there is survival after death. It was not, however, until the death of Sean that we were able to experience after-death survival for ourselves. Days after his death we were able to see his energy still with us, and when we asked him to move across the room the shimmering air would move and we could see the motion as well as follow his progress with L-rods. Our psychic friend could see and describe him clearly. Twelve years later Sean is still often with us as such a detectable presence, and always near as an internalized one. Both in life and in "death" this beautiful collie has been one of our teachers.

Animal friends who have died do sometimes visit their former homes, and it is a joy to welcome them. Brigit was always particularly pleased when her former housemates came to call. Animals, we believe, do go on after death as do people, and usually it is right for their attention to move on also. So do not be disappointed if your special friend does not seem to return to this plane, and do not try to bind a loved animal or person here. One has to love with open hand and heart.

We have mentioned how Brigit would show us changes in earth energies in the yard. Even driving in the car, when we crossed bands of harmful energy, she would get very restless and agitated. Because we don't feel that we have the right to request the removal of harmful entities or energies from places or from other people unless we have been asked to "pray" for them or have received permission from them to do so, and then have asked the three permission questions, we do not feel that we have the right to request changes as we drive down a road. But what we could and did do when traversing harmful energies was to request a protection from them. Brigit would then immediately settle down and stop her restless pacing in the back of our station wagon.

Part of Brigit's training of us was through our use of dowsing to care for her health. For example, we learned through dowsing that it was to her particular well-being not to eat dog food but to eat only natural "people food," and little by little, guided by our dowsing, she became more and more a vegetarian dog, eating cottage cheese, cheese, tofu, and milk for her protein. This is not to say that her diet would be correct for every dog, but for her particular highly strung nature, this food became what we dowsed as best for her. She ate three meals a day, including oatmeal and milk at breakfast, and a meal usually like our own at supper, but with extra protein and a little olive oil. In addition to this diet Brigit had help from two pioneering veterinarians. She got 500 milligrams of vitamin C daily in the vitamin combination formulated by Wendell O. Belfield (author of *How to Have a Healthier Dog*), to which we added extra vitamin E. Brigit also wore a special energy harness from Gloria Dodd, a holistic veterinarian from California. (The vegetarian diet was not suggested by either of these veterinarians but was based on our dowsing for Brigit, aided by the information in a number of publications on vegetarianism for dogs.)

With this combination of care, Brigit calmed down from a rather nervous puppyhood, her early skin and flea problems disappeared, and her coat went from rough to beautiful. We learned to dowse each meal that we planned to give her, as well as any additional supplements she needed that day.

A few times in her life she had sudden attacks of what appeared to be extreme fear. We would dowse for the problem and invariably at least one factor was the presence of a harmful-to-her spectral animal. We would ask permissions and request, as prayer, that this being be taken on to its next proper place of development, just as we would do for a harmful, formerly human entity. We would then give Brigit four drops of Bach Rescue Remedy in water—to drink if she would or, if not, rubbed on her nose and lips. Within a few minutes she would be fine again. Dowsers have found that such harmful spectral animals "on board" are often an important part of an animal's illness syndrome, so awareness of and learning to dowse about this kind of entity is an important way you can help your animal friends. The way you request the removal of harmful spectral animals differs from the removal of formerly human discarnate entities only in that it is your awareness of an animal's plight that must count as the initial request. Still dowse for the permissions, because spectral animals, like human entities, are sometimes here for good reason. Only those that are harmful are ones that you need to request to be helped onward to their next stage of development.

About fourteen months before she died, Brigit suffered a cerebral accident. Without dowsing, we would not have known what to do, and probably we would not have had those extra months of companionship and her continuing teaching of us. We asked whether it was the Divine Plan that she recover or whether it was best for her to be "put to sleep"; we dowsed that she was intended to be here longer. We made our healing prayers for her, just as we have described doing for a person. We also asked about all food and vitamins. Periodically we would dowse whether any of the usual methods of treatment would help her: allopathic veterinary, homeopathy, chiropractic, flower remedy, for example. We dowsed and sometimes used homeopathic preparations or a variety of flower essences for specific reasons. Bach Flower Rescue Remedy was particularly helpful in trauma and is a remedy for both people and animals that we would never want to be without. For a specific time we also dowsed and used a Pegasus Mugwort flower essence to assist in reestablishing synapses in Brigit's brain; from being in a state where she could barely stagger and was very confused, she quickly recovered her usual self.

When winter came we made Brigit a canvas sling harness so that when we walked outside we could hold her enough to keep her from falling in the snow. In the summer she went to Maine on vacation with us, although by that time she had to be carried up and down steps and onto the rocks by the sea. Her physical self faded gradually, but we dowsed that it was not her wish nor to the highest good for her to be "put to sleep." We increasingly needed to care for her and felt it a privilege to be able to do so. She lived until October, as we had dowsed she would, and in the last days of her life here finished her earth teachings by helping to introduce a young veterinarian to some ideas about the holistic care of animals. Then she left her beloved overcoat behind and went on to the next world. Like Sean, she still visits us sometimes, and we trust that we will continue to learn from her until we too go on to the next world.

We know that every curing is overridden at some time by death, yet we do what we can: all that we learned to do through dowsing certainly helped our beloved collie friends to have better lives here and also taught us a great deal. Brigit was nearly fourteen when she died, old indeed for a collie living in this part of the world. She was able to come back from trauma a number of times, assisted by the dowsing of what would help her and by healing prayers like those described in the preceding chapter. We tried always to keep clearly in mind "Thy will be done" and to accept that as the final authority on what would happen. But of course, in one sense, Brigit didn't really need "healing" at all; she was always a clear being, doing her intended work on this plane, which included teaching us. For that and for her joyful and loving friendship, we will always be grateful.

These few examples of learning through animal friends illustrate how, once you set out wholeheartedly on a path that combines dowsing with spiritual intention, the teachers and experiences that you need are given and the teachings need not come only from human beings. Sometimes lessons are very painful, but it is said that once having set out on a spiritual path, we get not what we want but what we *need* to grow and to do our intended work. It is up to us to find out what the lessons are in what we are given, to absorb them, and then with patience and trust to "get on with it."

We have very briefly described the kind of dowsing that one can do for a beloved pet. But often we want to do what we can for a wild creature—the bird that flies into the window, the baby squirrel rescued from a neighborhood cat. Sometimes ill and injured animals will seek out someone whom they feel to be kind or knowledgeable.

In order to be of help, we need knowledge. No help is given if we try to care for or feed an animal or bird in ways that do not meet its need. There are veterinarians and books to help, but when they are not available and you do not know what to do to help, you can dowse the answers to the questions you need answered, remembering to frame them so that they can be answered with a "yes" or "no." Will Rescue Remedy help? Is it best to leave the animal or bird alone? To bring it inside? Does its leg need a splint? Does this animal need a veterinarian's help? Is this bird ready yet to go back outside?

Studies have shown that the frequencies of birdsongs encourage plants to grow, a reminder of the symbiosis among nature's kingdoms.[39] Songbirds give us much pleasure as well, and we are distressed by their loss through cutting of forests, use of pesticides, and pollution. In cold northern winters, we can provide seeds and suet for birds; in summer we can plant bushes and vines and trees for later shelter and food and provide drinking water. In all seasons, we can try to protect them from predators. Humane societies say that an enormous number of songbirds are killed each year by roaming cats. Many cat owners thoughtlessly let out their cats without regard for the welfare of birds and small wild animals. Try to make your friends aware of this problem and also put your own feeding stations away from predator-sheltering bushes. You can also request that there be a protection for those creatures under your care on your property if you receive the permissions to do this.

Another aspect of our relationship with animals is what to do when they are present but you do not really want them to be—as when mice are in the house or squirrels are in the attic. Some dowsers attune to what they understand as the deva or governing intelligence of the animal species they are trying to contact and request that particular creatures be asked to leave the house; it is good to be able to suggest an appropriate alternative place for them to go. Some dowsers make the request in the form of a prayer. We can't really request that squirrels move out of the attic in the depths of winter, much as we might wish them to be gone, but when spring comes we can ask that they move out. The more attuned one becomes, recognizing the needs of both animals and people, it seems the better one's requests of this kind are heeded. One friend told of speaking to the earwig deva and afterward having all the earwigs leave her house. Terry Ross made a request in regard to spruce budworms in his wooded acreage in an area heavily infested and there were afterward no spruce budworms to be found on his property. This communication is surely a better way than harming a creature, which so often also means harming other creatures in the chain of life.

Communication with the devas has been much publicized

in writings that have come from the Findhorn Community in Scotland and more recently from Perelandra in Virginia. Devas are understood to be "overlighting" intelligences, each acting as a kind of group soul for a species or for a group within a species. A request to the deva is to the one in charge of or responsible for the individual animal or plant.

The books of Machaelle Small Wright of Perelandra tell of her gradual awareness of the nature intelligences who share space with us on this planet. These beings taught her how to garden in harmony with them; she uses for communication what we would describe as a form of dowsing, although she doesn't call it that.

Gardening can be greatly assisted through dowsing, as questions can be asked about everything from which seeds to order to where to plant. We remember Adele Dawson telling of a plant from the Southwest that was given to her. Carrying it, she dowsed where in her garden (in northern Vermont) it would like to be placed and she planted it there, where it thrived. Where a plant is to go, what companion plants are appropriate to be near it, its needs for water and fertilizer—all these are questions that can be dowsed. And plants do have consciousness and respond to recognition of themselves as individuals. Marjorie de Hartog described one experience she had with a little apple tree that belonged to a friend who lived some distance away. When she first made its acquaintance, it had been treated with "washing-up liquid" (dishwashing detergent) and looked very forlorn. Using her pendulum, she talked to it, helped to get it cleaned up, and dowsed to find out its name (as she had previously learned to do with plants), as well as to determine what treatment, if any, it needed. It turned out to be lacking several things, not the least of which was attention from its owner. Marjorie taught him how to dowse—he turned out to be a natural—and he visited the little tree every morning, using its name, communicating with it by pendulum to determine its condition, and soon it was fully recovered. Some months later Marjorie planned a return visit and her friend gave the good news to the apple tree, encouraging it daily as the date of her arrival approached. On the day she returned in mid-October the little tree produced one perfect apple blossom.[40]

To discover a plant's or animal's name, dowse through the alphabet to spell it out. Ask, "Please indicate the first letter by having the pendulum circle when I reach it. Second letter." And so on. We have known of a dog that completely changed its behavior for the better after its "true" name was dowsed and used. Some plants also like their real names to be known, and they do have distinct personalities and likes and dislikes that you can discover through dowsing. If a plant has a health problem, the appropriate therapy can be dowsed. Healing requests can be made for plants, just as they can for animals and people.

Christopher Bird's and Peter Tompkins's *Secret Life of Plants* and *Secrets of the Soil* detail many different approaches to understanding and using the powers of nature in a harmonious way. Ultimately, it seems that it is consciousness that determines what, among widely differing methods, does or does not work.

Improvement of the soil has proven to be of great assistance to the well-being of trees. *Secrets of the Soil* includes information on John Hamaker's method of using ground rock dust to revive ailing trees; the amount and kind of ground rock to use is something dowsers can ask. Harmful earth energies can affect trees, and studies have shown that trees appear to be harmed by transformers and certain other electrical fields.

On a piece of property there is usually a kind of "boss tree" in which the spirit of the place may reside. One may dowse for such a tree and, finding it, become its pupil. Sitting with your back to it, enter a meditation in which you can gradually experience the tree from within—"become" the tree.

It is said that if you make a bond with a tree, it will help you wherever you may be. Native Americans have a tradition of leaving cornmeal and tobacco when making a request of a tree. Jan de Hartog wished to do more. He learned to go onto a property, asking that he be led to a tree that needed his help. When he came to the tree, he would ask what help was needed. Sometimes it was physical—removing something that had fallen onto it, but sometimes it was a giving of energy to the tree—a kind of therapeutic touch—through his hands. He would ask, through questions to which he would dowse "yes" or "no," exactly what to do and for how long. Such a search for a needy tree can be done with dowsing rods or pendulum or through intuition alone, after dowsing for the permissions.[41]

An important action we can take toward healing the land is cleanup and restoration. This does not mean destroying what is wild—many traditions say that nature spirits need wild space of their own—but it does mean picking up human trash. It also means doing what we can to help restore or bring forth beauty and hope. Jean Giono wrote *The Man Who Planted Trees* (also called *The Man Who Planted Hope and Grew Happiness*)—the story of Elzeard Bouffier, a shepherd in Provence, who, working at his self-appointed task every day, during his lifetime planted great forests of trees that in turn brought water and lush growth back to areas of devastation. This fable has been a hopeful inspiration for many.[42] Real-life tree planters like Johnny Appleseed and Richard St. Barbe-Baker also come to mind. Let us do what we can in their spirit. We can ask permissions and dowse what would be appropriate to do and where.

All that we learn about earth energies through dowsing, and through studying geomantic systems such as feng shui, helps us to have right relationship with the land—to repair what needs to be repaired, to build only where it is appropriate to do so, and to honor the special places of the land. Where there is disharmony, when we have permission, we can pray for harmony. And finally, the more we learn to relate in brotherhood and sisterhood with all the kingdoms, the more our thought on the land, our breath itself, and simply our presence on the land will be healing to all around us.

We are all guests on this planet. We can learn to bring to our daily living the kind of collected presence and grace that we wish for in our visitors and hope to bring with us to the homes of our friends. Such an aware presence would appropriately express our gratitude for being able to be guests here for a time on this beautiful earth.

PART FIVE

TOWARD THE ONE: TOWARD STAGE SEVEN

✳

*When the mirror of your heart becomes clear and pure,
you'll behold images which are outside this world.
You will see the image and the image-Maker,
both the carpet of the spiritual expanse
and the One who spreads it.*[43]

—*Rumi*

*Just as your two eyes are under the control of the heart
and subject to the spirit's command,
all five senses move as the heart directs.
Hand and foot also move
like the staff in the hand of Moses.
If the heart wills, at once the foot begins to dance,
from neediness towards abundance.*[44]

—*Rumi*

15

THE SUPERSENSORY
WORLDS AND CREATIVE
IMAGINATION

In this chapter we consider dowsing as a means of access to supersensory worlds. By *supersensory* we mean realities available to us not through our conventionally thought-of senses but through a heightened sensory awareness that may also be thought of as intuitive. Following are four ways of thinking about supersensory realms.

First, there are fields that are invisible to most of us—such as auras of people, animals, and plants—but which we can feel pretty sure are there because we can dowse them and dowse changes in them. These dowsed responses also correlate with observations from those who can see some of these fields, and there are the beginnings of corroboration by instrumentation in this area. This is one kind of awareness of supersensory worlds—awareness of a field reality that is not generally known through the senses as we have been encouraged to develop their capacity in our society. Many people can see auras, however, and many more could learn to see them.[45] Young children often can see auras naturally—as they also can learn to dowse with ease. Often children can see the purple haze of energy ley lines that sometimes also appears on photographs of these lines. In some societies such abilities are accepted as a matter of course. But in our society these abilities are all treated as exceptional and somewhat suspect rather than natural.

Second, there are invisible kingdoms that are here with us. Some people can "see" invisible beings; others can learn to be aware of them through dowsing. Some of the most commonly "seen" or communicated with of these beings are devas and earth spirits.

A third way we interface with supersensory worlds is in the higher stages of dowsing. The ability to dowse for targets over-the-horizon or for information is part of the higher stages, but also when a dowser becomes enough in resonance with or attuned to the Divine Plan, there is the potential (in stages five and six) that a request—a prayer—may be made and "heard" and will result in changes on this physical plane. And for a few, such a degree of transparency may occur that the dowser may for a brief time live, move, and have his or her being in God and need only to bring a situation to mind to have changes occur reflexively (as in stage seven).

There is a fourth understanding of interaction with supersensory worlds, one that may not be so familiar as those mentioned so far. In *Magical Child Matures* Joseph Chilton Pearce wrote about postbiological development, intended in the Divine Plan to be a shift of orientation from the physical to the fluid mental world. Through this development our identity *apart* from brain or body manifests and becomes stable. Like all the developments before it, this step requires, in his paradigm, a model to which to bond—a safe place from which to make the next step. The spiritual bonding that this shift in orientation represents prepares the individual for life after death, when the physical body has been shed.

The Sufi master Hazrat Inayat Khan said, "The mind is a world, a world that man makes and in which he will make his

life in the hereafter, as a spider lives in the web it has woven."[46]
In this life we prepare for the next step, life after death. What
we realize of our divine inheritance in this life is what we take
with us after it is over.

Following the Siddha Yoga tradition, Joseph Chilton Pearce
used the idea of bonding to the model of the guru to help
contact the guru within the heart. Other paths have other ways.
In The Sufi Order tradition founded by Hazrat Inayat Khan,
there are concentrations on entering into the consciousness of
the masters, saints, and prophets of the major world religions.
The art of developing personality in this tradition is the art of
developing transparency so that Divine qualities may come
through and have embodiment on this earth plane. It is said that
the rust on the mirror of the heart needs to be removed—an
expression that began when mirrors were made of metal—with
"rust" being any obstruction that prevents reflection of Divine
qualities. Also, it is said in this tradition that we need to "die"
to limitation, to move beyond the boundaries we have imposed
upon ourselves, in order to begin the path of return toward the
Unity from which all manifestation flows.

In Henry Corbin's books on Ibn 'Arabi and other Sufi masters,
the world of Hurqalya is described. We may go to Hurqalya
after death; there, soul has a new body, but of a different
substance from the earth body we know. Hurqalya is described
as one of the planes or worlds beyond ours, and the appercep-
tion of Hurqalya is through *creative imagination.* This use of
"creative imagination" means a way of knowing this world
beyond before we die, and we both "create"—bring forth into
awareness—this world of Hurqalya and function in it through
the same creative imagination. In this lifetime we are intended
to learn to unfold creative imagination, and we feel that dowsing is an excellent way to develop this capacity.

We are accustomed to thinking of "imagination" as being

the same as fantasy, meaning "not true." But that is not how the word is being used by these writers or by us. Instead, it means unfoldment of sensory perception beyond the range that we usually think of as being possible. As Rumi says,

> When one sense in (the course of its) progress has loosed (its) bonds, all the rest of the senses become changed.
> When one sense has perceived things that are not objects of sense-perception, that which is of the invisible world becomes apparent to all the senses.[47]

In other words, once we have broken through the limitations we have accepted for our senses—those cocoons we weave around ourselves—our perceptions are able to move beyond the boundaries previously imposed by our limited sense of self.

We are familiar with the idea of visualization or imaging and the significant role discovered for it in healing and in creating what we think we want or need. But creative imagination, as we understand it, is not exactly this. Creative imagination brings forth into this world something that exists elsewhere, unfolding it coherently from the implicate order into the explicate order. In addition, the conditions we set up for receiving this gift determine the nature of the gift, much as our dowsing questions determine our answers. The function of creative imagination is to unveil what is real but hidden. In this way, creative imagination functions like intuition, which may be defined as resonance with what needs to be known.

A training in recognizing intuition, as apart from fear, wish, or self-delusion, is what a training in dowsing is or should be. In dowsing we program ourselves to receive true answers and to find specific targets, thus passing over anything that is not that for which we are asking. As we do this time after time, we train ourselves to develop true and accurate responses and eventually just to "know" an answer, which is intuition.

Creative imagination we understand to be true intuition but to go even further than the usual meaning of that term. When an experienced dowser is asking questions about a problem to be solved, a new thought or question sometimes occurs—gratuitously, synchronously—that will open up the inquiry still further, beyond the original understanding. Pursuing this lead—this opening of awareness—new information may be unveiled. As a dowser learns about subtle realms and begins to interact with beings from them, more beings make themselves known. As one proceeds on the dowsing and spiritual journey, more and more is unfolded to view, as the perceiving senses and capacities are changed and enlarged by the process. Spiritual literature is full of genuine experiencing of other planes by highly realized human beings through out-of-body episodes, bi-location, meditation, dreaming, or by other means. These realms are real, the experiences are real, but they are not to be understood through the usual paradigm of everyday reality. It is creative imagination that allows these subtle realms to be known. Creative imagination is the unfolding of those capacities that are part of the intended human development in life, but that reach beyond our usual sensory perceptions to illumine other realities, including those to which we move after physical death, thus helping us to know the purpose of our lives on earth.

In his comments on the Sufi tradition, psychiatrist Arthur Deikman notes:

> The ordinary man is said to suffer from confusion or "sleep" because of his tendency to use his *customary* thought patterns and perceptions to try to understand the meaning of his life and reach fulfillment. Consequently, his experience of reality is constricted, and dangerously so, because he tends to be unaware of it.

> Sufis assert that the awakening of man's latent percep-
> tual capacity (intuition) is not only crucial for his hap-
> piness but is the principal goal of his current phase of
> existence—it is man's evolutionary task.[48]

Where Dr. Deikman says "intuition," we would also include creative imagination, and dowsing is an excellent way to
begin to open capacity for both.

We live in the world of secondary reality and need to
function here; to do so we have created for ourselves a view of
reality that is actually very different from what the scientists now
tell us. Descriptions of our world in current physics make it a
place of wonders indeed, where nothing much is as we have
thought it is. Things are not what they seem to be, but still we
have developed a way of operating within this world of appearances. We sit on a stone and experience it as solid, even though
we know from physics that both we and the stone are mostly
empty space. We have to have a capacity for paradox to live
in this world, behaving as if there were a solid stone to sit on,
while also being aware that, on another level, what we experience here as solid is not "true." So we are prepared to know
that there is a magical quality to what appears at first anything
but magical. This acceptance of paradox can help us to realize
that what might previously have seemed entirely fantastic may
in truth be real.

Of imagination's creative power, called *himma* in Arabic—
the power of the heart—Henry Corbin wrote,

> When Ibn 'Arabi says that a gnostic *creates* something
> through his *himma*, through the creativity of his *heart*,
> he means . . . that the gnostic causes to appear, in the
> [plane] of the sensible world . . . something which
> already exists . . . in a higher [plane].[49]

He was referring to the perception of beings from the higher planes visiting this world in substantial form, but it seems that this same creativity of the heart may be what occurs when a dowser at stage six is able to request that something "new" come into this secondary reality and it does. This may mean an instant repair of a broken bone or new healthy tissue to replace diseased tissue.

The ability to bring about that kind of instant healing is of course still very rare, but we believe it is not only part of the human potential but part of the intention for the human being. Symbol, intent, and resonance are operational at the higher levels of dowsing, and the ability to be a catalyst for healing seems very clearly to measure the dowser's state of consciousness and spiritual unfoldment.

16

THE SPIRITUAL JOURNEY

The *mundus imaginalis* (imaginal world), of which Hurqalya is a part, is known by Sufis as a place we go after death—the celestial earth, shaped (as we understand it) for each person according to his or her worldview during life on the terrestrial earth. Included in that Sufi tradition is the idea that we proceed after death to ever subtler realms, acquiring in each realm a subtler aspect—one of more light—as we also leave behind a denser part. These other realms beyond death are still familiar because they are peopled by beings who appear something like what we know, although there are differences: for example, animals and trees and rocks may speak.

The idea of building the temple on terrestrial earth, common to the Abrahamic traditions—Judaism, Christianity, and Islam—and according to Mircea Eliade, to Eastern religions as well, is that it mirrors the temple that is part of and symbol of the celestial earth or spiritual realm. Each pillar, every measurement, each color has correspondences symbolic of that mirroring. The idea of rebuilding the temple is to reinstate on a forgetful earth those particular meanings that measurements, colors, and shapes evoke. The temple also means the individual body of a human being that is also intended to become the temple of God.

An idea in many traditions is that it is through mirroring that we approach bringing into manifestation that which we could become. By being able to see "what we could be if we would be what we might be," we are able to work toward that goal. Pir Vilayat Inayat Khan says that we "are always looking for ourselves in another being who is better able to manifest what we are than we ourselves have been able to do, so far."[50] All this corresponds to the idea of creative imagination, through which we bring forth something that already exists, and we have suggested that this may be understood as a bringing forth of qualities from the implicate order into forms within our explicate reality.

Remember that all views are hypotheses and may be considered as symbolic, metaphoric, and mythic ways of expressing relationships according to our understanding at the time. Yet it seems that contemporary descriptions of the nature of reality harmonize with ancient spiritual tradition. In physicist David Bohm's theory are the implicate and explicate orders, and yet beyond them is the Unity from which both come. In spiritual tradition there is also the idea of the One, unknowable, from whom streams the world of manifestation, the mirror through which the the Divine in part can be known. The understanding we have at this time is that we travel after this earth's lifetime to ever subtler realms until eventually, when it is our desire, we are united in the Oneness, but that this may be a long and gentle and loving process until we are ready for this ultimate recognition of What Is.

Tier upon tier of ever more subtle realms are described in some of the ancient traditions, leading many students of modern science to dismiss them, since they cannot understand where in the universe these realms might be. But even in ancient tradition are hints that these realms are at least in part inside us: what we learn is that everything without is also within.

We are helped to understand some of these difficult concepts of interior space as we progress as dowsers. When one learns to dowse earth energies, for example, one is recognizing the subtle currents of the earth first through the actions of the dowsing tools. After dowsing for a while, it is not uncommon for someone to be able to see a purple haze where an energy ley is. Likewise, as one learns about the subtle bodies and begins to dowse them, it becomes possible to see some of the envelopes that are the auras—perhaps first as haze but then later with colors. One can put oneself in the state of mind to see such things, but it is no use to strain for them; these abilities will unfold naturally when and if they are meant to do so.

After a while one may see shapes of discarnate beings or earth spirits. When this happens, one knows that this world is thickly inhabited by presences of which most people are unaware. This realization may help in understanding that many layers of ever more subtle beings may co-exist in the same "space" in entirely different but sometimes overlapping vibratory worlds. The subtle realms have not been considered in most scientific worldviews, any more than the subtle anatomy is recognized by most practitioners of modern allopathic medicine. This lack of recognition does *not* mean that the subtle realms and the subtle anatomy are not real and true. The increasing natural awareness that comes to dowsers can be a real help in their spiritual unfoldment because it gives them repeated experiences in recognizing the subtle realities of mystical traditions.

Learning to dowse in the manner we have described brings with it a growing awareness of connections and complexities within the various levels of being. More doors open with each phase of the learning so long as our conceptual system remains open-ended and is revised as needed.

On the path, we are given what we need in order to grow—

when our cups are not already full. Part of learning is learning to unlearn, to empty ourselves of what we think we know, of those unquestioned assumptions. It is not easy, however, to unlearn conditioned responses, for the mind has many ruts. We need to be aware of it when our thinking slips into a rut and to develop paths of access to *unconditioned* responses, which in part means unfoldment of our intuition.

We need to learn to live in the question. Dowsers know that they must focus clearly and without deviation on what is sought, but, more than that, they need to be clear about their role in the larger picture. Reshad Feild suggests that as we get out of bed in the morning, as our feet touch the floor, we ask, "May I be allowed to be of service this day?" It is clear to Whom this service is intended, although it is to be manifested in help in the world around us. Why do we want to know something? As Reshad Feild reminds us, "We breathe in only to breathe out."[51] Service must be the intention. With this focus clear, then we can begin to learn more precision in asking questions. Dowsing helps us to focus and articulate what it is that we need to know and do. By a marvelous synchronicity, once this process is begun with firm intent, it appears that the questions to ask come magically into the mind more and more often. Pathways are built up through authentic dowsing for this new kind of knowledge to come to us.

In a troubled world, dowsing gives empowerment to be able to be of help beyond the limitations our rational minds and our previous training might allow. To follow the seven-stage plan articulated in *The Divining Mind* and in this book is to become aware of the tremendous power of thought for good. It is the contention of many authentic dowsers that the higher skills cannot be used for non-good, and certainly an ethical stance is necessary to be able to move into those higher realms of dowsing in any solid and lasting way.

We have already seen that dowsing can be of help in practical matters. If you remain open and willing to learn, you will be able to think of many additional uses yourself. The awareness of complexity that dowsers develop also makes them more able to understand what happens behind the world of appearances. This awareness helps to remove the need for blame; we may not like what someone does, but we can learn to understand what factors have brought about those actions.

If we think of the world as a school, giving us the opportunity always to study something new, we can learn to transform our feelings of fear and inadequacy into something more positive by asking and exploring what qualities in us are being called forth by a particular challenge. Dowsing can be a useful tool in helping us to evaluate our experiences.

Learning to dowse can make one aware of the divine powers latent in all of us and of the path of service that allows what is latent to begin to manifest. One sees the potential dignity in all of creation and treats all creation as aspects of Divinity.

As awareness of the invisible worlds grows, trust in Divine Goodness that has created all that is also begins to grow. Fear is vanquished as one becomes aware that the essence of our lives continues after death.

For the beginning dowser all these things are down the road to note as stations to pass. Learning is certainly part of helping oneself toward spiritual unfoldment, but probably even more important is service, if it is true service and not ego inflation. True service requires compassion, empathy, resonance. Dowsers have many possibilities of being of service; this does not mean forcing our services on anyone but simply making ourselves ready so that, if we are asked, we will be able to do our personal best, without claims or any kind of bragging.

We remember the saying, "When you are ready, your teacher will appear." Remember that anybody or anything, any situation or any presence, may be a teacher. Our job is to be ready for what we are given—to become increasingly aware so that we are able to perceive the lessons when they come—so that when something speaks silently, we can hear. This means that we must learn to be increasingly present in the moment, which is another way of saying that we must learn to be awake and attentive to the world within and around us. Being mindful of the Unity beyond multiplicity while being attentive to the present moment is one way to describe the spiritual path.

17

THE INTELLIGENCE OF THE HEART

We begin the dowsing journey at stage one and then, matching understanding with practice, move slowly toward the seventh stage. The process cannot be hurried. At each stage there must be regular, verifiable practice to achieve mastery, and mastery of each stage is understood as preparation for the subsequent one. During the first four stages we think of ourselves as passive, learning to become instruments for receiving information of increased subtlety. We discover the importance of asking the right questions and of giving attention to what we do, and we are grounded in the present moment by the nature of the dowsing search. But as these four stages are mastered through service, we come to realize that we also function as transmitters. We learn to recognize our connection with all the natural kingdoms and the responsibility and relationship of self to all there is. In accepting a spiritual discipline, we begin to dissolve our sense of limited ego and to discover that there is the possibility of unbounded awareness. Using our dowsing skills and requesting always that "Thy will be done," we gradually may become instruments to help bring about harmony and healing in the world around us. Patiently, we unfold capacity as we "polish the mirrors of our hearts," knowing that the later stages of dowsing ability will occur naturally when and if God wills. We can only offer ourselves and do what we can at each stage to become ready to be of service.

The seven-stage path of dowsing is a useful metaphor for spiritual unfoldment. In this lifetime we are intended to discover creative imagination—intended to expand our perceptions beyond the range commonly thought possible—and that is what learning to dowse helps us to do: dowsing is a tool we may use to refine our ability to access intuition. Advancing with a spiritual focus through the stages described in *The Divining Mind* and in this book, we may also each be creating a more subtle body of light, in preparation for our next stage of life beyond that of this earth.

We consider the path of dowsing in the context of the subtle heart—understood to be at the center of all harmonious thought and action. Henry Corbin, that helpful guide to the complexities of the writing of Ibn 'Arabi, said that in the subtle body the "heart is the focus in which creative spiritual energy, that is, theophanic energy, is concentrated, whereas the Imagination is its organ."[52] We also recall Corbin's statement that the heart "produces true knowledge, comprehensive intuition, the gnosis . . . of God and the divine mysteries." He referred to the gnostic's heart as "the 'eye,' the organ by which God knows Himself, reveals Himself to Himself in the forms of His epiphanies."[53] William Chittick, writing about the work of Rumi, referred to the subtle heart:

> The ultimate center of man's consciousness, his inmost reality, his "meaning" as known by God, is called the "heart." . . . As for the lump of flesh within the breast, that is the shadow or outermost skin of the heart. Between this heart and that heart are infinite levels of consciousness and self-realization.

As man's inmost reality, the heart is always with God. But only the prophets and saints—who are called the "Possessors of the Heart"—have achieved God-consciousness, whereby they are truly and actually aware of God at the center of their being.[54]

Hazrat Inayat Khan said, "As soon as you knock at the gate of God, /which is your heart, /from there the answer comes."[55]

The subtle heart connects us with the universe beyond our physical selves. That place of correspondence between the physical and subtle hearts—the region between the physical heart and the solar plexus—Isha Schwaller de Lubicz called "the true tabernacle of the Divine Presence whose temple is the human body."[56]

Robert Lawlor wrote that in ancient Egypt, the achievement of the quality of understanding called "the Intelligence of the Heart . . . was life's implicit goal."[57]

Rumi wrote of this heart intelligence as:

A spring overflowing its springbox. A freshness
in the center of the chest. This other intelligence
does not turn yellow or stagnate. It's fluid,
and it doesn't move from outside to inside
through the conduits of plumbing learning.

This second knowing is a fountainhead
from within you, moving out.[58]

Through the insight of the subtle heart—the *intelligence of the heart*—comes the "knowing" of God, Who is mirrored in the Divine creation. Relationships exist among separate parts, but, through the subtle or spiritual heart, one may move beyond relationship toward Unity. If one can become even very briefly "the eye through which God sees" (comparable in our paradigm to the seventh stage of dowsing), one may become for that time a participant-observer, the dancer and the dance, in the play of Divine creation. Another way to say this is that there would then be no boundaries between love, lover, and beloved, or, as Rumi said, "There are no edges to my loving now."[59] Joseph Chilton Pearce wrote that if we are in this state, "We can only see *as God,* but then, when we do, God is all we can see."[60] This is the goal toward which we travel.

We like to think of dowsing skills unfolding through appropriate stages but always being centered in the heart. This does not mean "heart-centered" in a sentimental way, nor do we mean only in a loving, caring way—although of course it is that too—but we mean heart-centered in a way that acknowledges our commitment to the Truth—the origin and purpose of our life on earth and our home toward which we travel on the path of return. Joseph Chilton Pearce referred to love as "not a sentiment but a power, that intelligence of the heart that moves for our overall well-being.[61] His teacher told him that one must develop the intellect "to its highest possible extent, in order that it be a proper instrument of the intelligence of the heart. But only the heart can develop intellect to its highest extent."[62]

Pearce explained that if you isolate a heart cell, it will lose its rhythm and die, but if you put two heart cells in proximity but without touching, they will synchronize and beat in unison. There is a "cellular, chemical-hormonal kind of heart-intelligence." In addition, our hearts are guided by "a field of intelligence that is a larger, more universal, non-physical 'heart'— creative consciousness as itself." And there is "a final 'highest heart,' which moves us beyond all physical-emotional systems."[63]

The Divining Heart refers to dowsing centered in these understandings of the "heart" as they unfold in increasing subtlety.

If ever even briefly at the seventh stage of dowsing, we would be at one with That from which the intelligence of the heart flows.

We advance through the later stages of dowsing as if through a landscape that stretches beyond our horizon. We must then depend on the guidance of our individual heart compasses, our knowledge of the nature of the landscape, and the sense of inner trust that grows increasingly strong as our progress becomes verified. Eventually we may catch brief glimpses of our destination and feel a sense of nostalgia.

The further we travel, the more lightly we step upon the earth. We begin to recognize our relationship to this landscape and understand that we move to the same rhythms that give it form. As we climb upward, our view becomes wider and we see with increasing clarity that we are intended to move through awakening toward illumination. With a growing sense of joy, we realize that what we had thought at first was a new destination is the Source from which we first began our journey: the Light that has always been symbol of the wisdom we seek is the beacon for our return. That "subtle center of light," the heart,[64] resonates with that beacon, and the intelligence of the heart is the silent language of that Light.

Little did any of us know the length of the road when first we picked up those dowsing tools! May your journey be joyful, and, God willing, may the intelligence of the heart lead you home.

APPENDIX:
TERRY ROSS ON HEALING

The article below first appeared in the Winter 1988 issue of *The American Dowser* (Vol. 29, No. 1, 69–72) under the title "Sky Buffalo Speaks." "Sky Buffalo" is the name given to Terry Ross by Hyemeyohsts Storm. The approach to healing described has proven effective over many years.

Greetings to all members of the Society in the name of the Great Spirit and the four roads by which the One may be reached. May the feather of intuition and the sage of purification and protection that were a part of the little ceremony performed at the Annual Meeting in September attend you on the path, and may they continue as your steadfast guides. I would wish you the joy of the road, and a safe and successful journey.

Your wise counselor, whom we know and respect, has let it be known that it is time to bring out the facts of healing and to point out that absent or remote healing both summarizes the dowsing art and is its highest manifestation. I am in total agreement with that statement. The four roads acknowledged by Native Americans are the four planes of existence, the four levels of being, the four worlds of matter, sense, mind, and spirit that are part of everything that is and that are basic to the evolutionary scheme. The experimental physicists are beginning to touch upon these concepts with their theory of "strings," and the geneticists already accept disease as a disorder of the genes. Oncagenes, for example, are known to be activated by a mutation in one single subunit of the genetic material, DNA; and the DNA molecule, with its four-part double helix, is at once the product of this universal design and the assurance to us of our own participation in it. The Native American tradition speaks of this plan. The Grandfathers, from time immemorial, have always been prepared to share with those who were ready for it the knowledge and the enabling technique that would bring us closer to our destined roles of healer, cocreator, and companion to the Great Spirit.

Actions speak louder than words and anecdotes carry more meaning than theory. Allow me, therefore, to share with you a story that may illustrate what I would convey. Nature's way is to bring complementary parts together to form a whole, and so it is that one who has the technique to heal will inevitably attract those in need of it. So it was that a request came to one of our people, on behalf of a woman suffering from uterine cancer. Her husband stated that she had had three operations within fifteen days, that she was hospitalized in intensive care, and that the prognosis was bleak. At 10:05 A.M., immediately after receiving the request, a twofold regime was begun, first to remove all environmental influence of a damaging kind, and second to restore normalcy to the various levels of activity that we know surround and support the physical body. Thus, at her home three underground water flows, three encroachments from the astral plane, and three unusual electrical fields were detected. The entities were promptly escorted to those planes whence they could go forward under the divine plan and their influence erased from the woman's receptivity. The water veins were then altered so they could no longer attract wandering spirits in the future, and their "noxious" effect on the patient overcome. Similarly, the three electrical fields were rendered harmless to her. Three sites of exposure at the hospital, each involving water flows and spirit incursion, were treated in the same way, as well as five other such locations sought for and found in the pattern and routine of her normal life. At each geographical point further spirit-invasion was prevented and the woman's acceptance of emanation from those sources, as well as from the unsettling geopathic zones connected with them, was in that order denied. These sites of customary visitation in the present, together with sites from her past, were still potentially dangerous to her well-being in the hospital for the simple reason that no time or space exists on the subconscious level where memory can reproduce the effect of an absent cause. Examination of her past revealed such critical involvement with geopathic and spirit zones at points 3, 7, 8, 15, 19, 31, and 36 years before the present. All were processed and cleared as if they were current locations of destabilization, and as if they were active in the subconscious. The prenatal period was also scanned for such environmental damage, though none was found. There was, however, trauma originating with the shock of birthing, an almost inevitable finding in modern times. This, too, was dealt with, and dissolved and sealed from the repetitive power of memory. Thus, surely and completely, the patient was released from the totality of environmental impact to which she had been more or less continuously subjected throughout her life.

Having searched for and removed all environmental conflicts, the second step, as in all absent healing, calls for communication with the patient on the inner planes. It is conducted not on the astral or emotional level, but directly with the superior causal, or mental, body. This part of the biosystem is always open to such contact regardless of the state or condition of the physical body. In this case a gentle approach was made through time and space and a two-way relationship established, thus permitting the suggestion of hope and healing. Once confidence was developed, the more specific goal of a release of dross from both the visible and invisible bodies was proposed. The woman of our story reacted strongly to this, a sign of her latent vitality. The grounding of her negativity in the earth forces and consuming of it in celestial fire proceeded in an efficient manner. There followed the suggestions of forgiving all who had trespassed against her from the beginning of time, human or otherwise, of requesting the forgiveness of those against whom she had trespassed, and finally of forgiving herself. This prepared the way for a cooperative restructuring of the essential proto-atomic spins of her body and of the cells and tissue that had become disorganized. All was described and depicted, from the particular to the entirety, as being and remaining in harmony and balance. Finally, the suggestion of contact with her high source was made, with the addendum that the attitude and actions of her heart, mind, and body, as well as those of her professional advisors, her family, and her friends, be in conformity with her best interests under the divine plan. At this moment, at 10:33 A.M., she was released by the healer, with humble thanks, to the care and glory of the Great Spirit.

Several conclusions may be drawn from this regime, and I venture to list them as follows.

First, it is a regime that can be efficient at any distance and independent of time. It is effected by thought and thought alone, and implemented only after receiving permission on the conscious level. Second, it is effective because of a resonance factor—or what you call dowsing, albeit on other levels beside the physical plane. The basis for the phenomenon is one and the same, however, and can explain the activity on all of the levels. Resonance, it must be clear, can develop an entrainment, resulting in cooperation and even cocreation with the natural world. Third, it is assumed that there are differences in the awareness and development of the one seeking to be healed as well as the one attempting to heal, differences that can either prevent or facilitate the regime. The Grandfathers knew of this problem and solved it through the vision quest, which determined the correct path for the warrior, the hunter, or the shaman. Today, one might condition such relationships in terms of the unicameral as opposed to the bicameral brain; mind, however, in the Grandfathers' view, would always have remained distinct from brain and involve attunement and resonance with all the natural world, seen and unseen. Lastly, though I cannot speak for them, I think they would favor a sharing, with all who can accept them, of the things that were heretofore secret. All their prophecy points to a time of openness, of new understanding, and change.

In summary, the regime is predicated on a fourfold waveform that is the essence of all creation. It is a double helix that emanates from Allness, passing to the material through the three stages we call spiritual, mental, and astral. It is a wave with which man can resonate at any point of its spectrum, and wherever and whenever it is. The healer who exercises that power, upon receiving permission, can, with the speed of thought, identify any target of imbalance, disharmony, and disease, and through telecommunication bring about cooperative and remedial action. It is presumed that the spiritual level contains the blueprint of one's life and that the patient can be encouraged on the mental or formative level to conceptualize and activate that design so that its effect can be experienced on the astral and physical planes.

Implicit in the regime is the function of the three rings of the aura—the "biomorphs" that surround the physical body and are a matrix for it. The initial healing, it is thought, must take place in one or another of these rings, where the incipient disorder can first be perceived. All the familiar organs of our body appear to have their etheric counterparts in these surrounds, and can be observed there in whatever states they will eventually assume in the physical body. In every case the DNA, as the scientists are beginning to say, is the builder—or destroyer—and receives its commands from without.

As the Grandfathers taught us, it appears that we are all made from the same substance or life-force, and so in effect live with and for one another. The only limit to our cooperation or mutual healing is the degree to which we may be aware of that substance and its commonalty in all things. The resonance that makes healing possible is provided by organs in the material and immaterial bodies, an apparatus the Grandfathers knew well, and which they called "the magician's crest." It can immediately and accurately put us in contact with what we seek, including itself, for it too can be identified by the very means it provides. We have not found it because we have not looked for it, not believing in our own potential. It awaits our recognition and use, as indeed it was used in the case I have described.

This was an actual case, no more remarkable than hundreds

of others in which, against accepted odds, the woman fully recovered and is today without the cancer that was destroying her.
Recently on holiday, she is busy reconstructing her life with her
husband and children. She did not need or take chemotherapy.
Instead, on an inner level, she received twenty-eight minutes of a
specific and caring resonance. Technically her recovery might be
termed due to that resonance factor; others might say it was the
result of love.

ENDNOTES

Some material in this book was first presented in articles written for *The American Dowser* and in dowsing talks, including those as part of symposia (on "Dowsing and Consciousness," "Dowsing and Planetary Consciousness," and "Dowsing and Creativity") that we organized for the annual ASD dowsing conventions from 1985 through 1987.

PREFACE

1. Henry Corbin, *Creative Imagination in the Sufism of Ibn 'Arabi*, trans. Ralph Manheim (1969; reprint, Princeton: Princeton University Press, 1981), 221.

PART TWO

2. Pir Vilayat Inayat Khan, *Alchemical Wisdom: A Source for Intensive Inner Work* (Edmonds, Wash.: Unseen Oceans, 1991).

CHAPTER FIVE

3. David Bohm, *Wholeness and the Implicate Order* (London: Routledge & Kegan Paul, 1980), xi.

4. Itzhak Bentov with Mirtala Bentov, *A Cosmic Book: On the Mechanics of Creation* (New York: E. P. Dutton, 1982), 6.

CHAPTER 6

5. Joseph Chilton Pearce, "The Heart Connection," *The American Dowser* 26, no. 1 (February 1986): 26.

6. See Rupert Sheldrake, *A New Science of Life: The Hypothesis of Formative Causation* (London: Blond & Briggs, 1981).
7. See update of February 1983 article by Edith M. Jurka, M.D., "Brain Patterns Characteristic of Dowsers as Measured on the Mind Mirror," *The American Dowser*, 31, no. 4 (Fall 1991): 8–14.

PART THREE
8. From a letter appearing in the *New York Times*, 29 March 1972, quoted by Michael N. Nagler in *America Without Violence: Why Violence Persists and How You Can Stop It* (Covelo, Calif.: Island Press, 1982), 11.
9. T. Edward Ross 2nd, "The Resonance Factor," *The American Dowser* 28, no. 4 (Fall 1988): 8.

CHAPTER 9
10. Pearce, "The Heart Connection," 26–27.
11. Quoted by Reshad Feild in *Reason is Powerless in the Expression of Love* (Seattle: Chalice Guild, 1990), 60.
12. *We Are All Noah* is the title of Tom Regan's award-winning video, in which representatives of different religions speak about human responsibility to animals. Although we believe that a primary custodial responsibility for the planet is that of human beings, we do not discount the help of all the kingdoms concerned, nor the role of Gaia herself, toward preservation of the earth.
13. Henry Corbin, *The Man of Light in Iranian Sufism*, trans. Nancy Pearson (Boulder, Colo.: Shambhala, 1978), 81.
14. Pir Vilayat Inayat Khan, *Introducing Spirituality into Counseling and Therapy* (New Lebanon, N.Y.: Omega Publications, 1982), 53.

CHAPTER 10
15. Rumi. *Rumi: We Are Three, New Rumi Poems.* trans. Coleman Barks (Athens, Ga.: Maypop Books, 1987), 25.
16. See Mircea Eliade, "The Waters and Water Symbolism" in *Patterns in Comparative Religion* (New York: New American Library, 1974), 188–215; also Barbara G. Walker, *The Woman's*

Encyclopedia of Myths and Secrets (San Francisco: Harper & Row, 1983), 1066, and *The Woman's Dictionary of Symbols and Sacred Objects* (San Francisco: Harper & Row, 1988), 134, 341, 350–51, 356–57, 518.

17. Edward F. Edinger, *Anatomy of the Psyche: Alchemical Symbolism in Psychotherapy* (LaSalle, Ill.: Open Court, 1985), 80, 47. For further information on alchemical retreats, please contact The Sufi Order, North American Secretariat, P.O. Box 30065, Seattle, WA, 98103.

18. Theodor Schwenk, *Sensitive Chaos: The Creation of Flowing Forms in Water and Air*, trans. Olive Whicher and Johanna Wrigley (1978; reprint Bristol, England: Rudolf Steiner Press, 1990), 14–15.

19. Theodor Schwenk in Theodor Schwenk and Wolfram Schwenk, *Water: The Element of Life* (Hudson, N.Y.: Anthroposophic Press, 1989), 131. Drop pictures shown in this book are photographs of magnified movement patterns that appear when drops of distilled water fall onto water samples, setting them in motion. These forms indicate the quality of the water samples. Jennifer Greene of Waterforms, Inc., and Water Research Institute, Blue Hill, ME, 04614, has a drop picture laboratory, manufactures flowforms, and celebrates water through the creation of water environments. Originally designed by John Wilkes of England, flowforms are decorative sculptural shapes through which water passes with meanders and vortices; this patterning has been shown to enhance the quality of water.

20. See Olof Alexandersson, *Living Water: Viktor Schauberger and the Secrets of Natural Energy,* trans. Kit and Charles Zweigbergk (Wellingborough, England: Turnstone Press, 1982).

21. Reshad Feild, *Here to Heal* (Longmead, England: Element Books, 1985), 71.

22. Reshad Feild, "Spiral Vortex of Health," a talk taped at the American Society of Dowsers West Coast Conference, 1983.

23. Steven Halpern, *Tuning the Human Instrument: An Owner's Manual* (Belmont, Calif.: Spectrum Research Institute, 1978), 62–63.

CHAPTER 11

24. T. Edward Ross 2nd, in "Earth Energies: An Introduction to Their Study" by Patricia C. Wright, *The American Dowser* 26, no. 1 (February 1986): 53.

25. Craig F. Stead, from a dowsing talk.

26. Rupert Sheldrake, from a talk taped at Ojai, Calif., 1986.

27. Ibid.

CHAPTER 12

28. Joseph Chilton Pearce, *Magical Child Matures* (New York: E. P. Dutton, 1985), 21.

PART FOUR

29. Rumi, *Rumi: Daylight, A Daybook of Spiritual Guidance,* trans. from *The Mathnawi* by Camille and Kabir Helminski (Putney, Vt.: Threshold Books, 1990), 108.

CHAPTER 13

30. Larry Dossey, M.D., *Recovering the Soul: A Scientific and Spiritual Search* (New York: Bantam Books, 1989), 58.

31. Ibid., 59.

32. See E. H. Shattock, *Mind Your Body: A Practical Method of Self-Healing* (Wellingborough, England: Turnstone Press, 1979).

33. Dossey, *Recovering the Soul,* 53–54.

34. Ibid., 48.

CHAPTER 14

35. Ted Perry, *How Can One Sell the Air? Chief Seattle's Vision,* ed. Eli Gifford and R. Michael Cook (Summertown, Tenn.: Book Publishing Company, 1992), 32.

36. Peter Tompkins and Christopher Bird, *The Secret Life of Plants* (New York: Harper and Row, 1973), 136.

37. T. C. McLuhan, comp., *Touch the Earth: A Self-Portrait of Indian Existence* (New York: Promontory Press, 1971), 23.

38. Richard Gerber, M.D., *Vibrational Medicine: New Choices for Healing Ourselves* (Santa Fe: Bear & Co., 1988), 246.

39. See Peter Tompkins and Christopher Bird, *Secrets of the Soil* (New York: Harper & Row, 1989), 134–36.

40. Marjorie de Hartog in personal correspondence and in "Speaking to Our Condition: A Gathering of Friends," *The American Dowser* 29, no. 1 (Winter 1988): 68–69.

41. Jan de Hartog, from a talk taped at the 1986 American Society of Dowsers Convention, Danville, Vermont.

42. Jean Giono, *The Man Who Planted Trees* (Chelsea, Vt.: Chelsea Green Publishing Co., 1985). In her afterword Norma L. Goodrich says that Giono felt a writer is obligated "to profess hopefulness," which this beautiful book certainly does.

PART FIVE

43. *Rumi: Daylight*, 95.

44. Ibid., 86.

CHAPTER 15

45. To begin to see auras, ask a few people to stand against a light-colored background. Stand before them and observe their faces. If you had to say what color aura each has, what would you say? You will realize that this has nothing to do with skin color. Can you begin to see a faint haze around the heads? Seeing this haze around the head and body is often particularly easy to do when you are watching someone on a lighted stage. It helps to half-close your eyes as you look. You can learn to see auras around all living things, and of course you can dowse auras with your dowsing tools.

46. Hazrat Inayat Khan, *A Meditation Theme for Each Day: A Centenary Commemoration of the Birth of Hazrat Inayat Khan* (New Lebanon, N.Y.: Omega Publications, 1982), 20. See also the version in *Complete Works of Pir-O-Murshid Hazarat Inayat Khan, Original Texts: Lectures on Sufism, 1923*, vol. 2 (The Hague: East-West Publications, Nekbakht Foundation, 1988), 87–88.

47. Rumi, *The Mathnawi of Jalaluddin Rumi*, ed. and trans. Reynold A. Nicholson (1926; reprint, London: E. J. W. Gibb Memorial Trust, 1982), 2:389.

48. Arthur Deikman, M.D., quoted by Frances E. Vaughan in *Awakening Intuition* (Garden City, N.Y.: Anchor Press, 1979), 178.

49. Corbin, *Creative Imagination*, 226.

CHAPTER 16

50. Khan, *Introducing Spirituality*, 58.

51. Reshad Feild, *Breathing Alive: A Guide to Conscious Living* (Longmead, England: Element Books, 1988), 34.

CHAPTER 17

52. Corbin, *Creative Imagination*, 99.

53. Ibid., 221.

54. William Chittick, *The Sufi Path of Love: The Spiritual Teachings of Rumi* (Albany: State University of New York Press, 1983), 37.

55. Hazrat Inayat Khan, *Gayan* (New Lebanon, N.Y.: Omega Publications, 1988), 64.

56. Isha Schwaller de Lubicz, *The Opening of the Way: A Practical Guide to the Wisdom Teachings of Ancient Egypt* (Rochester, Vt.: Inner Traditions International, 1979), 59.

57. Robert Lawlor, *Sacred Geometry: Philosophy and Practice* (New York: Crossroad; London: Thames & Hudson, 1982), 14.

58. Rumi, "Two Kinds of Intelligence," version by Coleman Barks in *This Longing: Poetry, Teaching Stories, and Selected Letters,* versions by Coleman Barks and John Moyne (Putney, Vt.: Threshold Books, 1988), 36.

59. Rumi, "No Walls," version by Coleman Barks in *Night and Sleep,* versions by Coleman Barks and Robert Bly (Cambridge, Mass.: Yellow Moon Press, 1981).

60. Joseph Chilton Pearce, *Evolution's End: Claiming the Potential of Our Intelligence* (San Francisco: HarperCollins, 1992), 225.

61. Ibid., 210.

62. Ibid., 211.

63. Ibid., 104–5.

64. Corbin, *The Man of Light in Iranian Sufism,* 66.

RECOMMENDED READINGS

Books included here are ones mentioned in the text and others useful as background for ideas discussed; titles are listed under general headings, but often titles could be included in other categories as well.

Three titles are particularly helpful for understanding the general scope of this book. These are:

Corbin, Henry. *Creative Imagination in the Sufism of Ibn 'Arabi.* Translated by Ralph Manheim. 1969. Reprint, Princeton: Princeton University Press, 1981. On the nature of creative imagination as access to the supersensory worlds.

Khan, Pir Vilayat Inayat. *Introducing Spirituality into Counseling and Therapy.* New Lebanon, N.Y.: Omega Publications, 1982. An excellent introduction to a spiritual focus while living in the world. Omega Publications, Inc., RD1, Box 1030E, New Lebanon, NY 12125, is a source for many helpful books.

Ross, T. Edward, 2nd, and Richard D. Wright. *The Divining Mind.* Rochester, Vt.: Destiny Books, 1990. This is a dowsing school in a book.

I. THE REACH OF THE MIND
Background on the history of dowsing

Bird, Christopher. *The Divining Hand: The 500-Year-Old Mystery of Dowsing.* New York: E. P. Dutton, 1979.

Uses of Dowsing

The American Dowser. A quarterly journal published by the American Society of Dowsers, Danville, VT, 05828, which has many articles with practical information. In addition, ASD sponsors an annual convention in Vermont and regional conferences around the country, sells dowsing books and supplies, and, upon inquiry, will send you a packet of materials related to their activities. (Their counterpart in England is The British Society of Dowsers, Sycamore Barn, Tamley Lane, Hastingleigh, Ashford, Kent TN25 5HW, England.)

de Hartog, Jan. *The Centurion.* New York: Harper & Row, 1989. A fascinating novel that uses dowsing to unfold the story.

Farrelly, Frances K. *Search: A Manual of Experiments.* St. Petersburg, Fla.: Project Search, n.d. (Available through ASD.) Fran Farrelly is a master dowser who devised this manual of dowsing experiments for individual self-training.

Finch, Elizabeth and Bill. *The Pendulum and Your Health.* Sedona, Ariz.: Esoteric Publications, 1977.

Assorted Titles Related to the Uses of Dowsing

Becker, Robert O., M.D. *Cross Currents: The Promise of Electromedicine, the Perils of Electropollution.* Los Angeles: Jeremy P. Tarcher, 1990.

Becker, Robert O., M.D., and Gary Selden. *The Body Electric: Electromagnetism and the Foundation of Life.* New York: William Morrow, 1985.

Campbell, Don, ed. *Music: Physician for Times to Come.* Wheaton: Quest Books, 1991.

Dadd, Debra Lynn. *Nontoxic, Natural, & Earthwise: How to Protect Yourself and Your Family from Harmful Products and Live in Harmony with the Earth.* Los Angeles: Jeremy P. Tarcher, 1990.

Gimbel, Theo. *Healing Through Colour.* Saffron Walden, England: C. W. Daniel, 1980. One of the better books on color.

Halpern, Steven. *Tuning the Human Instrument: An Owner's Manual.* Belmont, Calif.: Spectrum Research Institute, 1978.

Hills, Christopher. *Nuclear Evolution: Discovery of the Rainbow Body.* Boulder Creek, Calif.: University of the Trees Press, 1977. Particularly interesting regarding personality differences among people with differing predominant aura colors.

Khan, Hazrat Inayat. *The Music of Life.* New Lebanon, N.Y.: Omega Press, 1983. Esoteric teachings on sound.

Pearson, David. *The Natural House Book: Creating a healthy, harmonious, and ecologically-sound home environment.* New York: Simon and Schuster, 1989.

Tame, David. *The Secret Power of Music.* Rochester, Vt.: Destiny Books, 1984.

Tansley, David V., D.C., *Radionics and the Subtle Anatomy of Man.* Saffron Walden, England: C. W. Daniel, 1982.

———. *The Raiment of Light: A Study of the Human Aura.* London: Routledge & Kegan Paul, 1984.

———. *Radionics: Interface with the Ether-Fields.* Bradford, England: Health Science Press, 1975, reprinted 1979.

———. *Radionics: A Patient's Guide to Instrumented Distant Diagnosis and Healing.* Longmead, England: Element Books, 1985.

Westlake, Aubrey T. *The Pattern of Health: A Search for a Greater Understanding of the Life Force in Health and Disease.* 1961. Reprint, Longmead, England: Element Books, 1985.

II. PARADIGM: A WAY OF THINKING
Scientific background

Ash, David, and Peter Hewitt. *Science of the Gods: Reconciling Mystery and Matter.* Bath, England: Gateway Books, 1990.

Bentov, Itzhak. *Stalking the Wild Pendulum: On the Mechanics of Consciousness.* New York: E. P. Dutton, 1977. Reprinted by Destiny Books, Rochester, Vt., in 1988.

Bentov, Itzhak, with Mirtala Bentov. *A Cosmic Book: On the Mechanics of Creation.* New York: E. P. Dutton, 1982. Reprinted by Destiny Books, Rochester, Vt., in 1988.

Blair, Lawrence. *Rhythms of Vision: The Changing Patterns of Belief.*

New York: Schocken Books, 1976. Reprinted by Destiny Books, Rochester, Vt. in 1991 as *Rhythms of Vision: The Changing Patterns of Myth and Consciousness.*

Bohm, David. *Wholeness and the Implicate Order.* London: Routledge and Kegan Paul, 1980.

Hayward, Jeremy M. *Perceiving Ordinary Magic.* Boulder, Colo., Shambhala, 1984.

Jurka, Edith M., M.D. "Brain Patterns Characteristic of Dowsers as Measured on the Mind Mirror," *The American Dowser* 31, no. 4 (Fall 1991): 8–14.

Sheldrake, Rupert. *A New Science of Life: The Hypothesis of Formative Causation.* London: Blond & Briggs, 1981.

———. *The Presence of the Past: Morphic Resonance and the Habits of Nature.* New York: Random, 1988.

Talbot, Michael. *The Holographic Universe.* New York: Harper Collins, 1991. An elegant overview of holography and its implications.

———. *Mysticism and the New Physics.* New York: Bantam Books, 1980.

Watson, Lyall. *Supernature: A Natural History of the Supernatural.* New York: Bantam, 1974.

Meditation

Fields, Rick, et al., *Chop Wood/ Carry Water.* Los Angeles: Jeremy P. Tarcher, 1984.

Khan, Pir Vilayat Inayat. For information on a taped course in meditation, write to The Sufi Order, P.O. Box 30065, Seattle, WA 98103.

LeShan, Lawrence. *How to Meditate.* New York: Bantam, 1975.

Ornstein, Robert E.. *The Psychology of Consciousness.* New York: Penguin Books, 1977.

Rama, Swami, Rudolph Ballentine, M.D., and Alan Hymes, M.D. *Science of Breath, A Practical Guide.* Honesdale, Pa.: Himalayan International Institute, 1979.

III. COOPERATION WITH NATURE
Planetary Consciousness

Corbin, Henry. *The Man of Light in Iranian Sufism.* Translated by Nancy Pearson. Boulder, Colo.: Shambhala, 1978. Helpful in understanding what it means to develop a body of light.

Feild, Reshad. *The Alchemy of the Heart.* Longmead, England: Element Books, 1990.

————. *Breathing Alive: A Guide to Conscious Living.* Longmead, England: Element Books, 1988.

————. *Reason is Powerless in the Expression of Love.* Seattle: Chalice Guild, 1990.

————. *Steps to Freedom: Discourses on the Alchemy of the Heart.* Putney, Vt.: Threshold Books, 1983.

Katz, Michael, ed., *Earth's Answer.* New York: Harper & Row, 1977. A collection of Lindisfarne Conference talks.

Lovelock, James. *Gaia: A New Look at Life on Earth.* New York: Oxford University Press, 1979.

Nagler, Michael N. *America without Violence: Why Violence Persists and How You Can Stop It.* Covelo, Calif.: Island Press, 1982.

Nasr, Seyyed Hossein. *Man and Nature: The Spiritual Crisis in Modern Man.* 1968. Reprint, London: Unwin Paperbacks, 1990. An important book on the relationship of the human being and nature.

Pearce, Joseph Chilton. "The Heart Connection," *The American Dowser* 26, no. 1 (February 1986): 25–28.

Robbins, John. *Diet for a New America.* Walpole, N.H.: Stillpoint, 1987. On the ramifications of our food choices.

Sheldrake, Rupert. *The Rebirth of Nature: The Greening of Science and God.* New York: Bantam Books, 1991.

Singer, Peter. *Animal Liberation: A New Ethic for Our Treatment of Animals.* New York: Avon Books, 1975.

Tompkins, Peter, and Christopher Bird. *The Secret Life of Plants.* New York: Harper and Row, 1973.

————. *Secrets of the Soil*. New York: Harper and Row, 1989. Health of the soil affects us all.

Whitehead, Alfred North. *Science and the Modern World*. 1925. Reprint, New York: New American Library, 1948.

Wynne-Tyson, Jon, ed. *The Extended Circle: A Commonplace Book of Animal Rights*. New York: Paragon, 1989.

Water

Alexandersson, Olof. *Living Water: Viktor Schauberger and the Secrets of Natural Energy*. Translated by Kit and Charles Zweigbergk. Wellingborough, England: Turnstone Press, 1982. On the nature of water.

The American Society of Dowsers. *The Water Dowsers Manual, 1963–1988*. Edited by Maria Perry. Danville, Vt.: ASD, 1990. Compilation of articles on water dowsing.

Eliade, Mircea. *Patterns in Comparative Religion*. New York: New American Library, 1958. Includes a section on the esoteric significance of water.

Rumi, Jalaluddin. *Rumi: We Are Three*. Translated by Coleman Barks. Athens, Ga.: Maypop Books, 1987. Many water images appear in Rumi's poems. There are a number of books of versions of Rumi poems by John Moyne, Coleman Barks, Robert Bly, and Edmund (Kabir) Helminski, all containing gems. We also highly recommend *Rumi: Daylight, A Daybook of Spiritual Guidance*, selected and translated from the *Mathnawi* by Camille and Kabir Helminski. Putney, Vt.: Threshold Books, 1990. (Other fine books are available from Threshold, RD 4, Box 600, Putney, VT 05346.)

Schwenk, Theodor. *Sensitive Chaos: The Creation of Flowing Forms in Water and Air*. Translated by Olive Whicher and Johanna Wrigley. Bristol, England: Rudolf Steiner Press, 1978. Reprinted, 1990. Beautifully illustrated, sensitive account.

Schwenk, Theodor, and Wolfram Schwenk. *Water: The Element of Life*. Translated by Marjorie Spock. Hudson, N.Y.: Anthroposophic Press, 1989. Includes some drop pictures.

Earth Energies

There is no single text that we can recommend to cover all aspects of the study of earth energies, but the following all offer pieces of the puzzle:

Doczi, Gyorgy. *The Power of Limits: Proportional Harmonies in Nature, Art and Architecture.* Boulder, Colo.: Shambhala, 1981. A wonderful book on pattern and proportion.

Feild, Reshad. *Here to Heal.* Longmead, England: Element Books, 1985. An important book on healing.

Lobell, John. *Between Silence and Light: Spirit in the Architecture of Louis I. Kahn.* Boulder, Colo.: Shambhala, 1979. This book contains profound statements on the nature of space and of light.

Lonegren, Sig. *Earth Mysteries Handbook: Wholistic Non-Invasive Data Gathering Techniques, a Joint Venture of ASD and NEARA.* Danville, Vt.: The American Society of Dowsers, 1985. This is Sig's understanding of earth energy dowsing, as is also his book *Spiritual Dowsing.* Glastonbury, England: Gothic Image, 1986.

Michell, John. *The New View Over Atlantis.* New York: Harper & Row, 1983. This is a classic text about earth mysteries, although it is not specifically about dowsing.

Miller, Hamish, and Paul Broadhurst. *Sun and Serpent.* Launceston, Cornwall, England: Pendragon Press, 1989. About tracking the Michael and Mary lines.

Pennick, Nigel. *The Ancient Science of Geomancy: Man in Harmony with the Earth.* London: Thames & Hudson, 1979. A basic text for understanding geomancy and very interesting—as are all Nigel Pennick's books—although not specifically about dowsing.

Rossbach, Sarah. *Feng Shui: The Chinese Art of Placement.* New York: E. P. Dutton, 1983.

———. *Interior Design with Feng Shui.* New York: E. P. Dutton, 1987.

Skinner, Stephen. *The Living Earth Manual of Feng Shui: Chinese Geomancy.* London: Routledge & Kegan Paul, 1982. A useful early book in English on feng shui.

Walters, Derek. *Chinese Geomancy.* Longmead, England: Element Books, 1989. An illustrated and accessible text.

IV. ATTENTION AND HEALING

Healing

Bach, Edward, M.D., and F. J. Wheeler, M.D. *The Bach Flower Remedies.* 1931. Reprint, New Canaan, Conn.: Keats Publishing, 1977. Basic book about the Bach Flower Remedies.

Dass, Ram, and Paul Gorman. *How Can I Help?* New York: Knopf, 1985. Excellent book about service.

Diamond, John, M.D. *Your Body Doesn't Lie.* New York: Warner Books, 1979. Basic kinesiology testing.

Dossey, Larry, M.D. *Recovering the Soul: A Scientific and Spiritual Search.* New York: Bantam Books, 1989. We also recommend Dr. Dossey's other books, including *Space, Time and Medicine.* Boulder, Colo.: Shambhala, 1982; and *Beyond Illness: Discovering the Experience of Health.* Boston: Shambhala, 1984. Published since our text was written is *Healing Words: The Power of Prayer and the Practice of Medicine.* San Francisco: HarperCollins, 1993.

Gerber, Richard, M.D. *Vibrational Medicine: New Choices for Healing Ourselves.* Santa Fe: Bear & Company, 1988. An overview of vibrational modalities, with implications even beyond what Dr. Gerber mentions.

Gurudas. *Flower Essences and Vibrational Healing.* 1983. Revised, San Rafael: Calif.: Cassandra Press, 1989. On flower essences and their assistance in healing.

Karagulla, Shafica, M.D. *Breakthrough to Creativity: Your Higher Sense Perception.* Marina del Rey, Calif.: DeVorss, 1967. A neuropsychiatrist reports on HSP (higher sense perception), including that of medical sensitives.

Karagulla, Shafica, M.D., and Dora van Gelder Kunz. *The Chakras and the Human Energy Fields.* Wheaton, Ill.: Theosophical Publishing House, 1989.

Khan, Hazrat Inayat. *Healing and the Mind World.* 1961. Revised edition, Katwijk, Holland: International Headquarters of the Sufi Movement and Servire, 1982. On the true nature of healing.

MacManaway, Bruce, with Johanna Turcan. *Healing: The Energy That Can Restore Health.* Wellingborough, England: Thorsons, 1983.

Neal, Viola Petitt, and Shafica Karagulla, M.D. *Through the Curtain.* Marina del Rey, Calif.: DeVorss, 1983.

Oneness of the Kingdoms

Belfield, Wendell O., D.V.M., and Martin Zucker. *How to Have a Healthier Dog.* San Jose, Calif.: Orthomolecular Specialities, 1993. For information on the book and on vitamin products, send $1.00 U.S. (or $2.00 U.S. if overseas) to Orthomolecular Specialties, P.O. Box 32232, San Jose, CA 95152–2232.

Boone, J. Allen. *Kinship With All Life.* New York: Harper & Row, 1976. We also recommend *The Language of Silence.* New York: Harper & Row, 1970. Both are beautiful books about relationship with animals.

Findhorn Community. *The Findhorn Garden: Pioneering a New Vision of Man and Nature in Cooperation.* New York: Harper Colophon, 1975. Pictures and text about the famous Findhorn garden.

Gore, Al. *Earth in the Balance.* New York: Plume, 1993.

Nicholson, Shirley and Brenda Rosen, comps. *Gaia's Hidden Life: The Unseen Intelligence of Nature.* Wheaton, Ill.: Quest Books, 1992.

Nollman, Jim. *Animal Dreaming: The Art and Science of Interspecies Communication.* New York: Bantam, 1987.

———. *Spiritual Ecology.* New York: Bantam, 1990.

Pitcairn, Richard H., D.V.M., and Susan Hubble Pitcairn. *Dr. Pitcairn's Complete Guide to Natural Health for Dogs & Cats.* Emmaus, Pa.: Rodale Press, 1982.

Roberts, Elizabeth and Elias Amidon. *Earth Prayers from Around the World.* New York: HarperSanFrancisco, 1991.

Rockefeller, Steven C., and John C. Elder. *Spirit and Nature: Why the Environment is a Religious Issue, An Interfaith Dialogue.* Boston: Beacon Press, 1992.

Stein, Diane. *Natural Healing for Dogs and Cats.* New York: The Crossing Press, 1993. With a foreword and appendices by Gloria Dodd, D.V.M., who is quoted extensively as well.

Swan, James A. *Nature as Teacher and Healer.* New York: Villard Books, 1992.

Uyldert, Mellie. *The Psychic Garden: Plants and Their Esoteric Relationship with Man.* Wellingborough, England: Thorsons, 1980. Like the Bird/Tompkins books, this one helps us toward more understanding of the plant kingdom.

Wright, Machaelle Small. *Behaving As If the God in All Life Mattered: A New Age Ecology.* Jeffersonton, Va.: Perelandra, 1987. Gardening in cooperation with earth spirits. See also her *Perelandra Garden Workbook: A Complete Guide to Gardening with Nature Intelligences.* Jeffersonton, Va.: Perelandra, 1987.

V. TOWARD THE ONE
The Supersensory Worlds, Creative Imagination, and the Intelligence of the Heart

Ardalan, Nader, and Laleh Bakhtiar. *The Sense of Unity: The Sufi Tradition in Persian Architecture.* Chicago: University of Chicago Press, 1973. Beautiful book about the use of pattern and proportion to express meaning.

Corbin, Henry. *Spiritual Body and Celestial Earth: From Mazdean Iran to Shiite Iran.* Translated by Nancy Pearson. Princeton: Princeton University Press, 1977. Includes material about the world of Hurqalya.

————. *Temple and Contemplation.* Translated by Philip Sherrard with the assistance of Liadain Sherrard. London: KPI in association with Islamic Publications, 1986. Henry Corbin's books are difficult but are very rewarding.

Khan, Hazrat Inayat. *The Sufi Message of Hazrat Inayat Khan: The*

Inner Life. Geneva, Switz.: International Headquarters Sufi Movement, 1979. One of a series of books made from transcripts of talks by this timeless ecumenical teacher who brought Sufi teachings to the West early in this century.

Pearce, Joseph Chilton. *Evolution's End: Claiming the Potential of Our Intelligence*. San Francisco: HarperCollins, 1992.

———. *Magical Child Matures*. New York: E. P. Dutton, Inc., 1985

Rumi, Jalaluddin. *The Mathnawi of Jalaluddin Rumi*. Edited by Reynold A. Nicholson. 1926. Reprint, London: E. J. W. Gibb Memorial Trust, 1982.

Vaughan, Frances E. *Awakening Intuition*. Garden City, N.Y.: Anchor Books, 1979. Includes the words of Dr. Arthur Deikman quoted in our text.